Your Impact is Your Superpower!

(No Spandex Suit Required.)

By Julie D. Burch

Dedication Page

This book has taken a long time to come to fruition. I have started it and stopped it more times than I care to count. So, first I need to thank Jesus for getting me through it. I will always pray that I write what you want me to write and that it always honors you first.

I want to dedicate this book to my family, my Mom, for being my first fan and getting me started in this speaking and writing business, you will always be my foundation. And my Dad and all my siblings, I love you all! And to my 6 amazing nieces, you all are my heart. You are all a big part of the reason I wrote this book. I hope you will read it and learn some of the lessons it took me way longer to learn. I pray for a lifetime of happiness for each one of you, never forget how much your Aunt Juju loves you!

To my rock star sister, Lorie. You jump; I jump. Always. Your willingness to counsel and guide and encourage me are only surpassed by your ability to make me laugh, the memes you find and send to me, and your knowledge of Elvis. Thank you, thank you very much.

And lastly, to my amazing, loving, supportive, and super-hot husband, Hank. I am blessed beyond measure to be your wife, and I will work every day I have left to make you proud and bring you joy. I never really lived until I met you and now my world sparkles. Love you more than you can possibly imagine, Handsome! Always remember, I Am Amazed by You! Free bird!!

Introduction

At the end of a long life, if you had to choose between impacting others and having great success for yourself, which would you choose?

When the question is posed, most of us would choose to have a positive impact on others. Our family, our friends, our community, even strangers. I feel that way as well. That is my mission and that is what this book is about. Ultimately, finding your mission to make an impact.

This book has been through many iterations over the last 20 years. I have started to write it and stopped more times than I can count. Even though it has had several titles and variations on the theme, it has always remained true to my one key guiding principle. You choose. It's your voice and your choice.

I kept coming back to making an impact because this is the heart of my mission on this earth. To positively impact those around me. It is different than leaving a legacy for me, quite frankly, because I always struggled with that.

It started one random Saturday night. My amazing husband and I were watching Alan Jackson videos on YouTube and the song "Small Town Southern Man" came on. It is definitely one of my favorites. Alan Jackson sings the line "your greatest contribution is the ones you leave behind." And even though I have heard that song and that line a million times before, for some reason this time it hit me. And I started to cry. I looked at my husband through my tears and said, "I don't have anyone I am leaving behind. I don't have any kids." He knows how sad this always makes me and how I have struggled with the idea of "leaving a legacy" even if it sounds irrational to some. He handled me like a champ, as always, and told me there are so many people I have influenced, including my 6 perfect nieces and my stepdaughter. It just didn't feel the same.

This is when I realized for me, it wasn't about leaving a legacy after I was gone exactly, it was about the impact I can make while I am still here. Now, don't get me wrong. Leaving a legacy is still on my to-do list. I believe firmly in having the estate plan in place to make sure my family doesn't have to go through any extra trauma when I go. Having a sister who is the most brilliant woman I know and an estate planning attorney makes that decision easy. But I needed to see something else. I needed to do something else. I wanted to make an impact on those around me now. And I realized, I can't be the only person who wants that. So why don't we? And how can we? That is what this book is about.

One of my favorite books in the Bible is the book of Jonah. I love this short but powerful story — not the way I learned about it as a kid in Sunday school, but what it means to me as an adult. Bishop Robert Barron, in his Word on Fire podcast, taught me two things. First, the story of Jonah is about finding your mission, and that speaks to my core. Second, that no one is given an experience of God without being sent. The first time I heard that, I thought, "Holy smokes, I am being sent! Sent to make an impact." So, here we go.

If you aren't familiar with the story of Jonah, he hears a higher voice — God's voice — and he is told to go to Nineveh and cry out against it. He is told to go west by land, and he goes east by sea. He is scared, it seems too big, too much, and he isn't equipped. But God doesn't send the equipped, He equips the sent. If only Jonah knew that earlier. Instead of listening to that higher voice, he runs the other way. He books passage on a boat to Tar shish. The opposite direction. Then what happens? This is the part most of us have heard. The storms come and threaten to sink the boat. Jonah realizes it is because he didn't follow his true path and tells everyone to throw him overboard so the seas will calm. And they do! That is when he is famously swallowed up by a great fish and saved.

When I break down this story and look at it in pieces, it makes so much sense. Think about it — we all have our mission. The impact we are meant to make on the world! We hear a voice tugging at us. It isn't always a loud voice, more often I think it is a soft voice. A voice so deep in our souls that we must be quiet and still to even hear it over the noise and chaos of our lives. But it IS there, and it is calling us to more. We know it, but like Jonah, we don't know what to do with it. So, we run the other way. We convince ourselves that it is too much, we don't have the time or the money, or whatever resource we can think have to justify why the voice is wrong and we just can't do it.

When the mission scares us or feels too overwhelming, we turn away. We turn away from the pressure of it, the responsibility of it, we turn away from the effort of even trying. But when we resist, the storms kick up. In Hebrew there is a term for it. It is called the *tohu vabohu* — what a great term! It basically means the watery chaos, the chaotic waters, and the storms of life. And isn't that the truth? When we are avoiding what we should be doing, we get caught up in the *tohu vabohu*, the chaos. It moves us further away from our mission. It confirms all the mental negativity we have been telling ourselves. All the reasons why we can't do whatever that mission is. It becomes a self-fulfilling prophecy. The more you tell yourself you can't do something, the more you convince yourself that it is true. The *tohu vabohu* takes over. Basically, when you are destined for more and you don't do it, you avoid it, you go the other way, the *tohu vabohu* kicks in. I'll bet I am not the only one who has felt that. Maybe you have too?

Then Jonah realizes the error of his ways and tries to make it right. Throw me overboard, I am clearly the problem! And if you throw me overboard then you will all be better off. And darn it all, they do it! They throw him overboard. But then, God. God sends the great fish to swallow him up. To constrain him. To constrain his willful resistance. I think it symbolizes a curative process. In times of hardship, depression, frustration, anxiety, self-doubt, whatever it is for you — on some level we understand the need to change. The desire for something different, something more. And when that realization hits us, the transformation begins. Change isn't easy, we will address that in this book, but it is doable. And when we listen to the higher voice, when we cooperate with that voice, cooperate with our purpose, oh the power we can unleash!

Just like Jonah. When he was swallowed up and constrained, when he prayed out of the depths, he was guided back to his mission, and was very successful to boot! He went to Nineveh and everyone repented. Pretty amazing what can happen when we follow our mission. The impact we can make is enormous.

We come full circle. I posed the question: "At the end of a long life, if you had to choose between impacting others and having great success for yourself, which would you choose?" I think Jonah shows us that we can do both. As a matter of fact, when we work to make an impact on others, when we follow our mission, our personal success naturally follows. My hope is that this book will help you do just that. Let's dive in!

Table of Contents

Chapter 1

Life Quakes & Emotional Earthquakes
(Why life falls apart sometimes—and why that might not be the worst thing)

Picture it. Long Beach California 2017. I was serving as the District II Vice President for the National Board of Directors for the American Business Women's Association. I stood at the podium in the conference room on the Queen Mary to give my speech and looked out at the hundreds of women in the audience. And in that moment the flashback hit me. I went back in time.

Long Beach was a pivotal place for me. 25 years prior I lived and worked in the same area, and it was one of the worst times of my life. At the time, I was in a relationship where domestic violence was the norm. I never knew when it would happen or what would set it off. I was constantly on edge, and I lived in fear.

It started out small. Little pushes, little shoves, a few slaps. And then it got worse. There were horrible episodes and fights. Bruises and black eyes. So many times, I said I was leaving. I knew I needed to get out. But every time I tried, he would tell me I wasn't capable. I wasn't smart enough or strong enough to live without him. It made me mad, but it also made me sad. What if he was right? And then he would cry and apologize, tell me he loved me and couldn't go on without me. I had to stay. He promised it wouldn't happen again. But it always did. I got tired of hiding the bruises and lying about where I got them. And then one random day, I was done. I couldn't do it anymore. I found out he was cheating on me with another woman. It had been going on for some time and now she was pregnant. He was going to be a dad, and it wasn't even my baby. I always suspected there were other women, but this was more than I could bear. I got out. I moved to Texas and started over. It was one of the best decisions I have ever made. A hard decision, but a good one.

Now, 25 years later I am back in Long Beach, standing on that stage on the Queen Mary speaking to that crowd of women. I had come so far! The realization of just how far I had come in that moment shook me like an earthquake. Or rather, a Life Quake. It was a huge Life Quake in my life. That was Life Quake number one.

I got out and got stronger. I did more and became more. Even though until that very moment in front of that very audience I don't think I realized it. In that moment I realized if I could do that, I can do anything! Think of the impact I can make in my life and in the life of those around me. And if I can do it, so can YOU!

Life quakes are a powerful thing. They are those moments in our life when something hits us. It evokes such strong emotions that we can feel emotionally overwhelmed when it happens. It runs through us like electricity, we feel it in every part of our heart and soul! It gives us a vision, a realization, a revelation. It makes us think.

It isn't always big Life Quakes. Sometimes it is what I call small tremors. Moments in our lives when we feel nudged. We don't always know who is nudging us or what we are being nudged to do, but we know something just happened to us. We have been called. But called to what? And how? Those life quakes and tremors are there to move us to action, to change our direction, to make an impact. We have all experienced the life quakes and tremors. Sometimes they come with perfect clarity, sometimes they come with complete confusion. We just want to scream "what does this mean? What am I supposed to do now?" It is up to us to figure it out. We must listen to those life quakes and tremors in our lives. Pay closer attention to when they happen and what is going on around us at the time.

That Life Quake shook me big at the time, but it took me some time to realize what action I needed to take. The lesson of this life quake was the realization that I am destined for more. That I am smart and strong and I can succeed. I have the God-given ability to change the course of my life and the impact that I make. I have power.

Life Quake two. March 22, 2019. My niece Adlee Louise was born. I am a very blessed Aunt. I have six amazing and beautiful nieces, and I love them all to the moon and back. But this was different. Adlee was the first one that I got to be a big part of her life from the beginning. I was included in it all. I went to a couple of doctor's appointments with my sister, I threw the baby shower bash to end all baby shower bashes, I was there at the hospital the morning she was born. That was a first. When she was born, I was the first one to hold her after her moms, of course. And the minute my sister put Adlee in my arms and I held that precious, perfect little girl, whew. HUGE Life Quake. Once again, I was shook. I knew at that moment a nudge was happening. Now it wasn't just about me. I had a bigger purpose in my life. I didn't just have to make an impact on me, or a difference in my life. I had to make an impact for her. For all my nieces. I was nudged to make a difference for them. I guess I do have a legacy after all.

I realized I am here to help others. I am here to make an impact on others who have ever felt unseen or unvalued. The impact I needed to embrace was the importance of equipping those around me to do the same. Make their impact, leave their mark. Now I understand and fully embrace that I exist to make a lasting impact on those around me, by helping people recognize their own power and value. (Mostly through my kick-ass keynote presentations, but hopefully through this book as well!)

When I speak to audiences, so often, I will be talking about the importance of growth and change and doing more or doing better in our lives. Periodically people will say they understand what I am saying, but they are good. They don't need to speak up when they are frustrated, bullied, or challenged. They don't need to say anything to that difficult person or in that difficult situation. They don't want to make any waves. They are what I call "It's OK, I'm OK people." They continue to say they are OK; they don't mind, they're a tree they can bend. They will take on the extra work or the extra problem or the extra anything because "it's OK." I am always called to remind them that it is absolutely NOT OK. It is not OK to be walked on or stepped over. Because it isn't just about you. It is about your kids, your nieces, my nieces, all those people around you that you have an impact on. You can tell your child they need to be confident enough to speak up, to share their thoughts, opinions, and ideas, that they need to be strong enough to speak out when challenged but if YOU don't DO that, what lesson will they ultimately learn?

Often, we fall into this behavior pattern because of exhaustion. Legitimately, we are exhausted, just tired of dealing with it. So, we don't. We throw our hands up and say, "It's OK, I'm OK." We convince ourselves we don't care enough about that person or that situation to say anything and we are just too tired to deal with it. I mean, how many times do I have to say something to that jerk?

Sometimes we fall into this behavior pattern because of a lack of courage. We are afraid to say anything because what if I make it worse? What if I look like an idiot, what if I get in trouble, what if I get fired, whatever the perceived worst-case scenario is that pops into your head at the time, and we decide not to act. The fear of the unknown is worse than the current frustration you are feeling. Our feelings aren't that important anyway, right? Or we are probably over-reacting, right?

But remember, silence is acceptance. Ultimately it isn't about you! It's about all those people who are watching. That is where the impact happens.

My Life Quake two hammered that message home. It was one thing for me to put up with poor treatment, but I would never allow that to happen to my nieces! If I wanted them to have the courage to stand up for what is right, then didn't I have to do that too? I needed to model the behavior.

There are so many examples of Life Quakes or nudges in my life, and I know your life too. It is not just the big life quakes, those smaller tremors can be equally valuable. You have had them too. Those moments in your life when you feel called to do more. The nudge that feels like someone is speaking to you.

We can't always identify the voice or where it came from. And sometimes it is just a faint whisper. But you know it was there.

It is the voices in your head. You know you talk to yourself, right? With my speaking schedule I travel a lot by myself. Sometimes I am the only one I have to talk to! But I digress. We do have voices in our head and that voice is not always the most supportive voice.

See, I have always had a lot of potential. Well, according to every teacher I have ever had! They wrote it in every report card I ever received from kindergarten through high school. They all said the same thing, "Julie has so much potential! If she would just apply herself." I hated that. Quite frankly, it scared me to death. What if I did apply myself and they were all wrong? What if I failed? What if I really didn't have that much potential after all? That little voice in my head was relentless. It continued to say to me "what if I fail?" over and over. Any time an opportunity for growth or improvement came along – or when I really needed to take a good look at myself in the mirror—that voice came back loud and clear. What if I fail? So, if I didn't really try, as long as I was a slacker and an underachiever then I never had to test the voice. Consequently, I didn't take a lot of risks, I lived quite simply in mediocrity. I never tried to improve or move forward or find success because, what if I failed? I was afraid to really apply myself or live up to my potential. Choosing instead to listen to that little voice. The voice allowed me to accept "less than" in all areas of my life. Relationships, work, finances, faith, everything. I was living in a grey space. Everything was stressful and I functioned feeling afraid most of the time. Afraid that the lie of my potential would catch up to me. I wanted something to be different, but I didn't know what and definitely didn't know how. But I longed for a life in Technicolor!

Then the tremor happened. It was a nudge. In one simple moment, for no apparent reason, the voice changed. It was quiet at first, I could barely hear it. It whispered to me. Instead of saying "What if I fail?" it whispered, "What if I soar?" Holy cow. And what if I do! What if I do? Mediocrity and the grey area were miserable, and I was ready to soar! Technicolor life here I come!

Whew, what an amazing revelation. I just knew the good life was about to begin! Then it hit, now what? What do I DO with this newly discovered belief? I had no idea where to start. But I had what started as a soul goal. It was a goal to move my soul!

I think that happens to so many of us. We know we should be doing something different, but we don't know what or even how to start. It happened to me, I'll bet it has happened to you too!

If you want something you have never had then you have to do something you have never done. You have to put down the old. Sounds so simple! And easy. In theory. But no, no it isn't. We have been doing the things we do for a long time; they are pretty ingrained in our psyche. They become so much a part of who we believe ourselves to be that they feel genetic. That is why we hear adults say all the time "that's just the way I am." Or "I have always been that way." And remember that little voice? That voice is so hard on us, it loves to tell us how bad we are at things. That voice will say "I'm so bad at. I am just bad at it. I have always been bad at it." The problem is this, the more you tell yourself you are bad at something, what happens? You are bad at it! It becomes a self-fulfilling prophecy. And I think once you have convinced yourself that it is so, you have to justify in your head why it is so. Then we will say things to ourselves like, "I'm just bad at it. I have always been bad at it. My Momma was bad at it too!" Again, like it's genetic! It's not, I promise. You can do something different. You must choose to do something different because you want different results. It starts with the mental shift.

Once you decide you want to get better or have an impact the next question is how. How do I do it? What now? So many people give up here. They don't know what to do so they do nothing. Most people are really good at being too busy to do anything new. They are so stumped by what to do that they fill their day with all the same things they have always done. Until they convince themselves again that they are just not meant to be successful or do anything more with their life. It is a cycle that repeats ad nauseam. I do the mediocre stuff and I get mediocre results. I have a tremor, a nudge that whispers I should do more. I think about it but don't know what that looks like or how, so I give up and go back to my mediocre life. Defeated again. How do we get off this hamster wheel?

You must believe you are more because behavior follows identity. When you believe you can, when you believe you are, then the behaviors can follow. The identity you have for yourself in your head is mission critical. If you continue to tell yourself you are not capable, your behaviors tend to follow. When you start to tell yourself, you are more and that you can do more, your behavior will follow that belief too. Changing your life starts with changing your mind.

Blaise Pascal, a French mathematician, inventor, scientist, and Catholic writer in the 1600's. He published a book in 1670, a collection of thoughts really. It was called Pansies. One of the thoughts or questions he poses is, "You want to have faith, but you don't know the way..." What do you do? He was speaking of his Catholic faith to people who were searching for theirs. You want to believe there is more, a higher power, but you can't seem to find it. It doesn't seem real to you. As a devout Catholic, he believed that when you struggle with your faith and you can't find the way, you must just behave in the way of the faith. Start to act by taking small steps.

I think we can use this same question here. You want to have an impact, but you don't know the way. You want to get better, but you don't know the way. You want to have more, be more, do more, but you don't know the way. Take small steps. It doesn't have to happen overnight, but you must take a step.

For so many of us it's not only that we don't know what action to take, we don't even know what our bigger purpose is. Forest Gump asks his Mama on her death bed, "What's my destiny Mama?" and she wisely responds that is up to him to figure out. Life is like a box of chocolates, you never know what you are going to get. She always knew how to say things. It's true, our destiny is for us to figure out. Our destiny is at the intersection of what we love, what the world needs, and what our talents are. When you can find that sweet spot, you are golden! If you struggle with this, please know, I do too! Still, to this day I question myself, am I doing the things I am being called to do? Am I working toward making a difference for those around me? And then I try to refocus and say a little prayer that I am doing the right things, and it is so important that I keep moving forward. Focus on what is important. I can't say that enough. To myself and to you! Because where we focus is where we go.

I didn't get married until I was 37 years old. I never thought I would get married. Not because I had anything against the institution of marriage, I just thought I was a career girl. I was really focused on my speaking business and just didn't care about dating or marriage. So, I dated very little. It was a joke in my family that I canceled more dates than I went on. My Mom called every guy I dated Brad, because why bother to learn his name? He wouldn't be around very long. When I met my husband to be they were a little skeptical to say the least. As a matter of fact, my sister lost money to my mom when I didn't cancel my first date! His name is Hank not Brad by the way, and it took me some time to get them to remember that. But Hank changed my life. Talk about a life quake! I knew pretty quickly I was smitten! I always described him as my rugged outdoorsman. He drove a big bright red Ford truck. As a retired firefighter, I don't think the red truck is optional.

I remember early on, I would be driving around the Dallas area where we live, with him always on my mind. And then I started seeing bright red Ford trucks EVERYWHERE! Do you know half of the DFW metroplex apparently drives red Ford trucks? Now, that can't be true, of course. So why, all the sudden, did I start seeing them everywhere? Because I was looking for them. I was looking for him. What you focus on is what you see.

Try this quick exercise. Right now, wherever you are, look around and count the number of things you see that are red. Take a minute and count.

Now stop, close your eyes and think of everything around you that is yellow. Can you think of anything that is yellow? It's highly likely the answer is no. There are probably plenty of yellow items around you, but you weren't looking for yellow! It really is true, what you focus on becomes your reality. You get more of what you focus on.

Think about how true this is for people. There are plenty of people out there that only see the negative. They see all the bad stuff, they are very quick to tell you all the things that not only can go wrong but will inevitably go wrong. They always see the bad. There was that great character in Saturday Night live played by Rachel Dratch, Debbie Downer. Such a funny take on this concept! The more negative things she pointed out the more negative things happened to her. This is true for you too. The more negative you see, the more negative you will continue to see. What you focus on, you tend to get more of it is the way it goes. The great thing about this is that it works the other way too! If you focus on the positive you will attract more positive! Mindset matters. Henry Ford famously said, "Whether you believe you can or you believe you can't you are probably right." I love that! It is so true! So, what do you believe? What do you WANT to believe?

You have experienced the life quakes and the tremors in your life. You know you are destined for more; you just know it. And this doesn't mean you have to find the cure for child cancer, go to Mars, or invent the post it note! Our impact isn't always in big giant things. As a matter of fact, they almost never are. Our impact is in small things. It's the moments when we leave a ripple. The moments we may not even realize happened. It is in the consistent behavior of living a life of caring and compassion and integrity. It is giving everything you have to everything you do, that is how true impact happens. It is living your life every day in the best way possible. It is giving your best at work and at home even on the hard days. It is the small things, I promise. No cure for cancer required.

The crazy thing is, we don't always know when we make a difference. We don't always know who is watching. And let's be honest, we may never know. In my business this is so often true. I have had thousands of people in my audience, and I don't get to chat with all of them afterward or even six months or five years down the road. I must give everything I have, leave it all on the stage every single time because I believe that someone hears me. I believe there is someone out there that I had an impact on. And you do too.

I had only been speaking professionally for about five years; I was new to the speaking game. But I will never forget this day. I was teaching a full day stress management session. This is one of my most in demand keynote presentations and one of my favorites to this day. I had a great day and a great audience! We learned a lot but I am pretty sure we laughed a lot more! When I wrapped up the session, I was feeling pretty good about the day, I thought it went well. I was exhausted, I knew I had definitely left it all out there. I had a woman come up to me afterward. She waited until most of the other people had left and she approached me quietly with big tears in her eyes. She told me she needed to tell me something. She shared that she had just lost her husband of 25 years only 2 weeks before the seminar. She was devastated and really did not want to come but her sister encouraged her to just show up. She shared that she was significantly younger than her late husband, so even though she knew someday, he would probably go before her she wasn't prepared for it. I mean, who would be? She said she was so very much in love and she really didn't believe she could go on without him. She told me with tears in her eyes that she believed that she would never be able to laugh again. Ever. And today I made her laugh. She said she really laughed, deep belly laughs, and she was so grateful for that. I was stunned. She said I changed her life but all I did was be myself and do my job. I did what I was called to do, and I made an impact. Then I started crying too! We cried and we hugged. I don't think she has any idea of the impact SHE made on me that day. She has no idea about the ripple effect she had on me. I promise you to this day, if I ever have a day when I am not feeling up to giving it my all and I think about just phoning it in, I think about that woman. And I remember that I might make an impact on someone today and I better be ready for it. Impact doesn't have to be big, newsworthy, front-page things. Sometimes it is making a woman laugh.

Making an impact can be taking the time to do all things with love. It is listening when people need to be heard. It is taking the time when you don't think you have the time to give. It is doing what is right when no one is there to see you do it. It is always speaking with love and kindness about others. I know, I know, that is not always the most fun thing, but we all know I am right here. That is when we have the biggest impact. It will change your life because you will feel better when you do better and it will impact others because of the ripple you are leaving. I still don't know that woman's name, but I will never forget her. And I hope she remembers me too. She made an impact.

Chapter 2

Spoiler Alert: Change Is Required

(Because doing the same thing over and over is not a personality trait)

We have established change is required. One of my most requested keynote presentations is on dealing with change. I think of it as harnessing the power of change. I think of it like this because when change is harnessed and intentional it can be a force to be reckoned with. Too often though, change isn't intentional. It is instead reactive and forced, often by others or circumstances. On the other hand, when change is proactive and intentional it will have a positive impact, not just on us but on others.

Life in general is just rampant with change. So how we navigate that, how we feel about it, how we mentally prepare for it, what we do to be better at it, I think matters. So, I'd like you to think about the changes in your life. Think about a change that you have been through in the last year, or a change that you know is coming in the next year. My guess is everyone can think of something. Whether it is a recent change or a change that you know is on the horizon, change is a constant. And if you are reading this book, I hope you are planning some big changes in your life! If that is all true, then this information is obviously relevant to everyone. Change is not going anywhere. You've been through it, you're gonna go through it, it's out there. How we think about change today is different than how we approached it in the past. Some of you may remember, back in the day, the way we used to handle change, was we kind of just sat back and tried to wait it out. We would hold on to our desks and try to come in under the radar so we might come out unscathed on the other side. Our goal was to "get through it."

Where we are today is different. We don't get through to the other side of it. It's not about change anymore. It's about a continuous evolution. We are constantly evolving. I have a visual picture in my head that I always think of with this, you are running in a race. I know, I don't seem like a runner but go with me here. So, you're running in a race. You get to the finish line, and you think, "Yeah! I finished it!" Then you look down, and it says, "Finish line, right after that, it says 'starting line.' "You are starting all over. It's a constant evolution, so we're not getting through it anymore. We can learn how to navigate change in our lives more effectively if we are willing to put in the effort. How do we do it? Here are some thoughts.

There are three areas of change that we can talk about. I want to give you some thoughts on all three of these areas so you can take back control and have an impact in all three. The three areas of change are internal change, current change, and future change.

The first area of change is internal change. Internal change is the mental side; it's in your head. You may have already figured out that most of our issues with change are all in our heads! How do we get ourselves mentally on board with change? That's the internal side of change. Then we have what I call current change. Those are the changes that are happening right now. You are in the middle of it. It's in process. It's happening as we speak. And I oftentimes feel like these changes are the ones that were thrust upon us, not necessarily something we chose. Sometimes it is, but oftentimes it just feels thrust upon us. And then, of course, future change, because if we can acknowledge that it's not really about change per se, it's about a continuous evolution, then we must understand it's not about just getting us through what we're dealing with now, but it's preparing us for the future change, for the continuous growth and development.

Internal Change.

Let's start with the internal change. I have 6 amazing nieces and as I have watched them all grow something struck me. For kids, we celebrate all the changes! We celebrate their first word, their first step, their first birthday smash cake! We celebrate it all. And then what happens as we get older? All of a sudden, we stop celebrating. How often have we heard people say that they don't even want to acknowledge their birthday? We don't want to grow anymore or at least get older. It's interesting to me as we get older, we feel that way.

When I present this topic as a keynote presentation, I use an exercise that has become one of my favorites of all time. I call it the change game. Now, I understand you are reading this and can't exactly do the exercise, but I am going to walk you through it and I want you to use your imagination and think about how you would respond and how you would feel at each step.

I challenge everyone to play along with me and stand up and face a partner. And I say, just look at your partner. Look them up and down. Check them out. Could you pick them out of a police lineup if you had to? Imagine yourself doing this... Then I tell them, now that we have all that weird stuff out of the way, here is what you will do. I want everyone to turn around so you're not facing your partner. You don't have to touch backs or do anything weird. Just turn around, so you are not looking at your partner. Now, I want you to change three things about yourself, Go. Once they have done it, I tell them to turn back around and see if they can identify the three changes their partner made. They laugh, I laugh, and it is fun to watch! Then I tell them for part two, I want you to turn back around and change three more things. Remember, you are doing this in your mind too, how are you feeling? What are you thinking? Then of course they have to turn back around and identify the new three. They are definitely getting more creative and laughing a lot now.

I like to tease them a little and say, "Now for part three..." and after they moan about it, I tell them they can sit back down! Now, think about it. What could we possibly learn from that exercise? There are plenty of smaller lessons that can be identified. They can learn to pay attention to the small things, that change can be fun, that change isn't always even noticeable to others. All those things can be true. But of course, there is something more. Something much more! I will tell you what I absolutely love about this exercise. Seriously, I absolutely adore it, because I think that in this exercise, as ridiculous as it can feel, we get to witness exactly what happens in the change process. So, let's rewind.

I said, change three things about yourself. Did you hear or feel the tone of the room? The whole room basically said arghhhhh.... In unison! They said things like "three things! I don't have three things! What am I supposed to change?" While they are complaining I ignore it. I let them complain. And once they do that, they start to do it. They start making changes.

Something I've observed, and this is just my own personal observation and doing this exercise a bunch of times, is that in the first round, I see a lot of people taking things off. People take off their jewelry, they take off their glasses, and they take off their watch. And I think that's interesting. An interesting perception of what we tend to think about change. I believe it's the perception that when change is required, we are going to lose something.

Then I made them do it again, I said, "Part two change three more things." Holy cow, y'all should hear the room then! The universal arghhhhhhh, gets even louder and the reasons they can't do it grow louder and more prevalent as well. "I don't have three more things! This is going to be naked training!" After all the complaints and the groans, guess what happens? Everyone starts to do it. They come up with three more things. I find people get even more creative and come up with different things to change. I've seen people put their shoes on opposite feet, put their jacket on backward, their glasses on the back of their head. People put their hair up and down, all kinds of new hairstyles happen in the crowd. Are those things still change? Absolutely. I think that's so important to acknowledge, change doesn't have to mean we are losing something.

It is also to acknowledge that we all have feelings about change. And it usually starts with the groaning, arghhhhhh. It is a natural reaction, and it is normal.

Think about it. The audience knew, just like you knew, what we were talking about. You knew the topic was change. I promise you, if I had stood up and said, "So, how many of you like change? Y'all probably would have thought, “You know, I do. I know a lot of people do not like it, but I do. I recognize that that is how we grow and how we get better.” Everyone is all in when the question is asked. But when I ask you to actually change three things, the universal response is generally, arghhhh! And you know what? I think that is okay. I don't think it's about the “arghhhh,” I think it's about what we do after the arghhhh. I think if we allow that feeling, that initial reaction to happen, its okay. If we are willing to move past it, because it is a human emotion. And let’s face it, reactions to change are linked to emotion. What's the number one emotion that we would associate with change? Fear, yes, Fear. That's the number one. But here's the thing about fear. Fear is an underlying emotion. It's a deep down emotion. But that's not the outward emotion we tend to see. Most people tend to mask that underlying emotion. I'd be willing to bet money that not one of you reading this has ever been in a team meeting of some sort, and someone stood up and said, "Okay, y'all, there's going to be a change in policy, change in system, change in structure." And somebody in that meeting said, "Oh, I am very fearful." Who says that? No one. They mask the fear, generally with a stronger, manly emotion.

Emotions like anger, frustration, and defiance. They angrily say things like, "Oh, here we go again. Great. This is ridiculous. We tried this three years ago, and it didn't work then. It won't work now. This is terrible and I hate it." We mask the fear, but of course, fear is ultimately the underlying emotion. Because of this, we must allow ourselves, and allow each other, the initial arghhhh, knowing we are going to move past it.

I have no idea where I first heard it, but one of my favorite sayings of all time is, "When the pain of change is less than the pain of staying the same, you'll change." Isn't that true? So powerful. Of course, for our purposes we don't mean physical pain. We mean emotional pain or even mental pain. Let's face it, we have already agreed that the emotion associated with change is fear, because change is an unknown. What exactly are we afraid of? Well, it can be a ton of different things. The fear of the unknown, what if we fail. What if we can't do it, what if we look stupid doing it, what if it makes us irrelevant, and all those fears deep inside our head. They are scary and a mystery. Which in turn makes the pain of staying the same seem less scary. And let's face it, people stay in places even when they are unhappy because at least it is a known feeling. We have all known people, maybe we have even been that person that stayed in a bad job or a bad relationship because it was less scary than changing and doing something new. You hate your boss but what if you leave and your new boss is worse? At least you know what kind of awful you are getting every day where you currently are. And all your friends have told you that guy you are dating is a jerk, and you know it too. But at least you have a date on national holidays. And what if you never find someone new?

Keep in mind though, we all have a tipping point where all of the sudden, the pain of change feels better than the pain of staying the same. It really is getting mentally to that tipping point, so we can reframe and reimagine change. It's not about change as a transaction, or change is a moment, or change is an event. It's about that continuous evolution. It's about growth and development. And that is uncomfortable. We must learn to be comfortable being uncomfortable.

There's a great story about a Rabbi, Dr. Abraham Twerski, who was sitting in a dentist office and saw a magazine article posing the question "How do lobsters grow?" His first thought was he didn't care, but then became interested. Reading the article it said that lobsters are mushy, soft creatures that are inside a rigid shell. That rigid shell does not expand. So, how does the lobster grow? Well, as the lobster grows the shell becomes too confining and uncomfortable, the lobster then goes behind a rock formation to protect itself from predatory fish, casts off its shell and produces a new one. Eventually that shell becomes confining and uncomfortable as it grows so the lobster repeats the behavior. This happens numerous times. The stimulation for the lobster to grow is feeling uncomfortable. If lobsters had doctors they probably would never grow! They would go to the doctor, and the doctor would give them some Valium or Percocet and they would feel fine! They would never grow.

We have to realize that times of stress are also times that are signals for growth and if we use adversity properly, we can grow through adversity.

It's all about being just a little bit uncomfortable, because that's where the growth happens. That's the internal side of change. It requires a mindset shift. I always say you must reimagine change. You choose to see it differently.

Current Change.

Let's dig a little deeper on current change. For those changes you are currently dealing with or even starting because of this book. I want to give you four ideas, things to consider, maybe marinate in it for a bit to fully embrace these ideas to help you navigate those current changes more effectively.

First, work where you have the power. That means focus on what you control. What do you control? Yourself, right? You control your mindset, you control your reactions, your responses. There are two key things we control: our attitudes and our actions. You are going to see this again when we talk about grit and resilience because it is all related.

Attitude.

You control your attitude, meaning how you choose to approach things. As a leader, wanting to make an impact, the people around you are looking to you. Your family, friends, co-workers, employees, even customers. They are watching how you handle change. What do you say when change is presented? When those processes or those systems or things evolve, how do you handle it? These people are looking at you and they are modeling the behavior that you're leading by. Think about your kids, they watch everything you do and listen to everything you say! Every reaction you have. I know I shouldn't have, but I couldn't help laughing a little too loud when one of my amazing nieces at 5 years old cussed! I looked at my sister because we both knew where she heard it!

I have a friend who is a teacher. I remember her telling me that she could tell how her students' parents talked about school because it was generally reflected in the way her students talked about it. If you gripe and groan about how hard it is getting up and getting them ready in the morning, if you complain about all the school supplies you have to buy and how the school should provide them, those messages are all being received loud and clear.

This always reminds me of the crab mentality. If you aren't familiar with this it is the craziest thing ever! And completely true.

When the fishermen go out on the boat to catch crab, they bring them up in these big crab traps. And they must keep them alive, if you kill them you have to immediately freeze them. So, the fishermen bring them up on the deck of the boat, and they put them in these big baskets or buckets. They fill those baskets all the way to the top. Which means the crab on top could totally escape! All they would have to do is jump down, skitter across the deck of the boat, and jump back in the water! I picture them yelling "Freedom!" on their way down to a big splash!

They could get away. But they do not, why? Because the crabs below them will not let them. This is true. The crabs below them will hold them down. They will grab them with their pincher; they will break their legs before they let them get away. They will stab them and kill them before they will let them escape. Apparently, these crab's mindset is, if I'm stuck here so are you! As soon as I heard that, I thought, "I have worked with that woman." You know who I am talking about, you have worked with her too! That one person who likes to bring everybody down. The negative, complainer, faultfinder that just wear us out. It is all about attitude. Two things, first, don't be the crab. Nobody likes you. So, if that is you, knock it off. Stop being that person, nobody wants to deal with you.

I also think, especially as impact makers, how we come together, how we empower each other makes a difference. We must hold each other accountable to a higher standard. That means we can't have crabs around us.

We must regulate that. We must make different choices about the people we give our time and energy to. It is OK to keep people at a distance that don't feed the positive in your life. It is called setting boundaries, and it is not easy, but it is required. Sometimes it's people that are the closest to you, family or friends. But if they aren't supporting you and your positive attitude and the good choices you are making for your life, it may be time to get some distance. It doesn't mean we have to cut people out of our lives completely; I understand that it feels difficult, even unrealistic or a little mean. It is not mean though, it is for your own sanity.

I have a strict no crab policy in my life! If you are going to be negative and crabby you are going to get very little of my time and energy. I want to spend my time and energy on the things that help me grow and be successful. Fill the space around you with positive, encouraging people that inspire you to do more! Trust me, holding yourself accountable makes a huge impact on those watching.

Actions.

When our desire is to be an impact maker, your actions matter. Part of embracing change is about our desire to maintain relevance. Just like companies and organizations must always continue to stay relevant we as individuals need to do the same thing!

Congratulations to you for reading this book, because that is exactly what you are doing! You are growing your skills and expanding your impact. Well done!

My favorite example of the importance of staying relevant in business is Blockbuster video. Y'all remember Blockbuster video? If any of you are about my age, I won't tell you what that age is... but well, you understand! If you were in high school in the eighties, then you know what I'm talking about. We loved Blockbuster Video! That was the place to go on Fridays and Saturdays! Holy cow, we would do our hair, we would put on makeup just to go to the Blockbuster. We were not just looking for a movie. We were looking for somebody to watch it with! What happened to Blockbuster? They went out of business because they didn't change, they didn't stay relevant. They kept that same business model the whole time. And think about the world changed around them. All of the sudden we have Red Box and Netflix. Remember back when Netflix would mail you DVD's? We thought we were living large! And now it is all streaming.

The whole time Blockbuster stayed the same. They were looking at people like me sitting back and going, "Don't worry, girl, we got you." Come on in and meet someone while you pick up that VHS tape. I know I am probably not the only one who was glad Blockbuster shut down so we didn't have to pay off those late charges we still owed.

Now, think about how those of you, especially have been doing the same thing for a long time. I think about the nursing profession as an example. People that have been nursing for 10 years, 20 years, even 30 years, think about the changes they have seen.

Think about the things that they might have done in the beginning of their career that are no longer acceptable. Even things that we would probably be appalled that was normal. When I read this, I nearly fell over. During the Civil War, when somebody would get shot, for example, at that time they didn't have the medical knowledge or technology to fix that, so they just cut the leg off instead. And they would amputate a leg right there next to the battlefield! They would have you do a shot of whiskey and bite on a stick. Could you imagine if nurses today rolled you into the operating room and told you to do this shot of whiskey and bite on a stick and the doctor will be right in. I mean, could you imagine that? Because that's no longer relevant. We must continue to grow our skills, to constantly be evolving if we want to be an impact maker. Our attitudes and actions are where we have the power and that is what we want to keep our focus.

The second idea to help you navigate current change is understand your why.

There's a great line in the movie 12 Strong, I am moved by it every time. There is this powerful moment at the beginning of the movie when the commander is sending out his team to fight in Afghanistan. They are the first team to be deployed in this way after 9/11. The commander gives him a piece of the destroyed World Trade Center and tells him, "The most important thing a man can take into combat is the reason why." Holy cow, that gets me every time.

I find when we understand our why, things become much easier. I share this story with you and I am sort of embarrassed by it. I always say I don't like being this vulnerable because it makes me look bad and I want you to like me. However, it is my truth, it is my testimony, and I have to tell it. So, this is true confessions, I used to be a smoker. If you're a smoker, no hate, I've been there. Although, my caveat is, I quit almost 20 years ago. But I was a smoker.

When I smoked, I was one of the mean smokers. I was one of those defiant smokers. People told me all the time, "Those are goanna kill you." And my response was, "I'm gonna die anyway!" "You should quit!" and I would blow smoke right in their face. I was terrible! I had one person tell me that "You know every cigarette you smoke takes 7 minutes off the end of your life" And my response was "I didn't have anything planned for those last seven minutes anyway!" Man, I would get mad. And then my dad got sick. Man, I loved my dad. My dad had been a smoker, and when he got older, he had COPD and emphysema, and he had very limited use of his lungs.

It was hard watching my dad get sick. I watched as he got sicker and sicker. Toward the end, he had to have oxygen all the time. He had one of those big oxygen machines in his house that had, like a 900 mile cord so he could get around the house. But he got to a place where he couldn't climb a flight of stairs or even fly to come see me in Texas. He could barely walk across the living room without getting winded. And I watched him get sicker and sicker. And what I realized watching that was... I was not afraid that cigarettes were going to kill me. I was afraid they wouldn't. I was afraid I would have to live like that. And when that hit me, I was done. I threw away all the cigarettes I had left and I never smoked another one. And I wasn't tempted, there was never a moment I "almost" did. I knew my why. I was absolutely clear on that why. When you know your why, those decisions become easier. What's your why? I think we all have a personal why, you need to know what your personal why is. What is the reason you get up every morning? Why do you put your feet on the ground and get going? If you can be very clear on that everything in your life becomes easier. Your why gives you direction and makes every decision you make every day easier.

When the days get difficult, the days get hard, and the days get long if we can remind ourselves of our why, we have clarity.

We said focus on what we can control and understand your why. The third thing to deal with current change is take small steps.

Take small steps.

The third thing is to take small steps. I find this so funny and very true, we are all or nothing people. It's cultural I suppose. We are all in or all out, there is no in between. Go big or go home! You are in or you are out, that is a very common mindset.

I was presenting a keynote presentation for a group of about 150 people. I had a woman raise her hand and share this with the entire room. She said, "I hate my job. I hate it. I'm miserable. I dread going into work every day. I work with evil people." She said "My boss is the spawn of Satan!" That was my favorite part. Now, when she said that, I said, "Whew!! That sounds bad. You better quit."

Now, when I said that, you can imagine what she said. She said, "Well, I can't!" And I looked at her and said, "But it sounds so bad. Why not?" And Y'all know exactly what she said. What she said was really funny. She said, "I have children! I have to put food on their table, a roof over their head, and shoes on their feet!"

I said, "Amen, sister!" I get that and it makes a lot of sense. I bet a lot of you can relate to that. She fell victim to the wrong mindset. She had decided for whatever reason that in her life she only had two choices. Either option one, she stayed and worked at this pathetic miserable job for the rest of her pathetic miserable existence or option two, she quit tomorrow and was homeless, living on the street, and her children had no shoes! I would like option three please! There has to be something in the middle. It's not all or nothing, for Pete's sake.

I think it is very similar to hot buttons. I am sure you know what I mean by hot buttons. People know how to push our buttons.

To me, it's like when we were kids. I grew up in a big family. I have four brothers and a sister. My brother Jeff is 13 months younger than me. Although, I am sure he looks much older! Don't tell him I said that. When we were little, we really never fought. We really didn't to this day, we are very close. But as kids, he used to do that thing, he would put his finger really close to my face, and he'd say, "I'm not touching you, I'm not touching you!" I'd get so mad. I'd run to my mom, "Mom, Jeff's not touching me!" He makes me so mad. And my mom would look at me and say, "Julie, Jeff doesn't make you mad. You let him make you mad." That made me madder! I hated that! And if she could hear me, I would never admit this, but she was right, wasn't she? If I wanted Jeff to stop, what did I have to do? Hit him! Or walk away. Whatever. All the peace loving people. Ultimately, I had to do something different. As long as I continued to do the same thing, I was going to continue to get the same result. And you all that is true for every single one of us, isn't it? If you want something to be different in your life, you have to do something different. And it doesn't have to be giant leaps and bounds. It can be small steps. We get caught up in the all or nothing mindset and decide that whatever it is, it must be impossible. Stop telling yourself what you can't do and start figuring out what you can do. What small step can you take? Action is momentum even if it is small actions. Take small steps.

Number four, as an impact maker, you must lead through change. You must lead through it. We have already addressed the fact that every person you work with, live with, love, is looking to you for your guidance. We all tend to look around and wonder, how are they responding? How are they reacting? How are they feeling? To be a true impact maker it is crucial that you lead through the change in a positive way.

When we can handle the mental side of change, we can reimagine change, and we can think of it as a continuous evolution rather than an event that we have to get through, we do it differently than other people and we make an impact.

What are you going to do to lead through the changes in your life? What are some things you can do?

The last thing, and this is quick, because this to me, is super simple. There are two thoughts that I want to share about future change. First, I already shared the idea that when you get to the finish line, immediately after is a new starting line. Change isn't going away. So, what do we do? You must be proactive rather than reactive. If all we do is sit back and then react to what's happening around us, we are not going to be as effective. But when we can be the person that leads through it, or you look for ways that we can grow, then you lead that charge, you're being proactive, not reactive. And we make growth normal. Second, I think we should look for ways to make changing normal. Every day with little things, make it normal. Drive home from work a new way, try a new recipe, and go to a new restaurant, anything you can do that is just a little different. It doesn't have to be giant things, remember small steps! When you do little things differently every day you make changing normal. Then when the big things come along it is not as shocking or difficult, it is just par for the course. We can smile to ourselves and remind ourselves that we have got this! Because we have been practicing it for ages. We become an impact maker by leading the change. And remember, you have totally got this!

Chapter 3

Eyes Forward, Drama Backward

(How to stop living in reverse)

My mom used to tell the story about what it was like teaching my youngest brother Jason how to drive. She said she would be sitting in the passenger seat watching how dangerously close to the curb Jason was driving. You know the feeling when you sort wince, squish up your face and peek out of one eye because you see the problem, or in this case, the curb coming right at you? She was a good Mom and didn't want to overreact and make Jason more nervous, so she would calmly say, "Jason, watch the curb." And he would respond, "OK, Mom, I am." And he would still get closer, so again, "Jason, watch the curb." And again, "I am!" Then all of a sudden, bam! He hit the curb! As my mom shouted, "I told you to watch the curb!" Jason, in a very frustrated tone snapped, "I WAS!" and you know what? That is exactly what he was doing.

The more he looked at the curb the closer he got to it. It is like the law of attraction.

Have you ever decided you are going to buy that new car you have been eyeing? The perfect blue Mercedes, for example. As soon as you have made the decision you start to see blue Mercedes everywhere!

When I first started dating my now husband, I was smitten pretty quick. And for a woman who had no intention of ever getting married and barely dated, this was a new thing for me for sure! He drove a big bright red Ford truck. He is a retired firefighter after all, so the color was required. I will tell you what though, as soon as I realized I was pretty crazy about this guy, I started to see big red Ford trucks everywhere! It seemed like everyone in the entire Dallas-Fort Worth metroplex drove red Ford trucks! Or is it possible, there were not any more red Ford trucks on the road than there were before, but instead I was focusing on something so intently, it was just sitting in front of my brain so that was what I kept seeing?

This is a very real concept. Imagine a cyclist barreling down a narrow trail in the woods. They're weaving through trees, flying past rocks and branches, their hearts pounding with adrenaline. Ask any experienced cyclist what the key is to staying upright and moving forward, and they'll tell you: focus on where you want to go, not on what you want to avoid.

The moment your eyes fix on the tree trunk in your path, your handlebars will follow, and sure enough—you'll crash right into it. That was what was happening to Jason. Every time he heard "watch the curb," his eyes and the steering wheel led him right there. Focus on where you want to go not where you are avoiding. So, if you keep your gaze on the opening between the trees, your body will naturally adjust, and you'll glide safely through.

Life works much the same way. Where we focus, we go.

Too often, our eyes are glued to the wrong things: regrets from the past, fears of failure, bitterness over disappointments, or even the comfort of old successes. Instead of steering toward the clear path ahead, we end up circling the same obstacles again and again.

This book is about making an impact in the lives around us. And here's a truth worth holding onto: impact doesn't happen behind us. It's created in the steps we take forward.

But forward movement isn't random, it requires guidance. And that guidance comes from something deeper than impulse, emotion, or convenience. It comes from values.

Why We Can't Live Backward

One of the biggest barriers to living a life of impact is the temptation to dwell on the past. We replay mistakes like broken records, we linger in what-ifs, and we hold onto grudges that weigh us down like stones in our pockets.

Living backward might feel safe because it's familiar, but it's also paralyzing. Let's look at a few ways this shows up:

Regret

We all have chapters of life we wish we could rewrite—words spoken in anger, missed opportunities, broken relationships, and times we chose fear over courage. Regret can be a good teacher, but it's a terrible master. When we live in regret, we trap ourselves in a story that's already finished instead of writing the one still in front of us. We tend to hold on to that regret, that past mistake for so long, it often becomes a part of who we think we are. Then we say things like, "I can't help it, that's just how I am." When we convince ourselves that it is just our personality, that it is just who we are, then we give ourselves permission to stay that way forever. We firmly decide that those negative feelings, situations, missed opportunities, or whatever they are, unfortunately, are destined to define us forever. This is such a bad way of seeing things. We can't ignore our past mistakes but the most important thing we can do is make better decisions going forward. There is absolutely nothing you can do that will change the fact that Jesus loves you, and aren't we supposed to love like Jesus? Maybe it should start with how we treat ourselves.

Nostalgia

Nostalgia seems gentler than regret, but it can be just as dangerous. It's the temptation to keep looking backward to "the good old days." When we glorify the past, we lose our hunger for what could be ahead. It's like trying to drive with your eyes locked on the rearview mirror—you'll never notice the new road opening in front of you. We don't want to end up like Al Bundy from the television show Married with Children! The high point of his life were the four touchdowns he threw in a high school football game. At some point we need to step up and create a new impact, it's not about what it was like back in the good ol' days, the best days are in the future! You have to take back control and choose what the future is going to look like and what impact you will have on those around you. And we will never get there if we insist on living in the past. Focus forward.

Shame

For many, the past isn't just regret or nostalgia—it's a source of shame. And shame has a way of whispering, "This is who you are. You'll never move beyond it." But that's a lie. Shame glues us to yesterday, but values invite us to tomorrow. The feelings of inadequacy can sneak up on us and attack when we least expect it. When I was 16 and got my driver's license, I was a terrible driver. Seriously, terrible. I had two accidents and three tickets before my 17th birthday. I know, my poor Mom! I was a "challenge" for sure. But here is the thing, I am a great driver now. Granted I am a wee bit older. OK, a lot older. But that little voice in the back of my mind that told me I was a bad driver didn't go away for many years. And sometimes the people around me liked to mention it with some good-natured ribbing, but it was a source of frustration for me for many years. I had to learn to let it go and focus forward. I might have been a poor driver but that is not who I am now. Embrace the present and the future and let the past live right there, in the past!

Pride

Even success can trap us. When we define ourselves by past victories, we may stop growing, stop learning, and stop risking. Pride says, "What I've already done is enough," while impact whispers, "There's more ahead."

The Danger of Backward Living

When we dwell on the past, we rob ourselves of three essential things. First, clarity, meaning we stop seeing what's possible. Second, courage, meaning we lose the strength to try again. And lastly, contribution, meaning we miss the chance to influence others with our growth.

To put it simply: backward focus wastes energy. And energy is one of the most valuable resources we have.

The Power of Forward Focus

So, if we can't live backward, what's the alternative? We live forward. Forward focus is not about ignoring the past; it's about learning from it, then facing what lies ahead with purpose. To me, this is all about recognizing that hope is what lives ahead!

Hope, by definition, is forward-facing. It's the belief that something better, truer, stronger is possible in the future. No one says, "I hope yesterday changes." Hope is always about tomorrow. And without hope, we lose the fuel for impact. Focusing forward is choosing hope. It's saying, "What's in front of me matters more than what's behind me." And this is a key life skill for people of impact.

Small Steps Matter

Sometimes, the idea of "focusing forward" feels overwhelming. We picture giant leaps, dramatic reinventions, or overnight success. But in reality, forward motion is almost always about small, consistent steps. A single honest conversation, a decision to forgive, a daily practice of aligning with your values, or a choice to take the next right step, even if the entire path isn't clear.

Big impact is built on the foundation of small steps. We are going to dig deeper into this in chapter 7.

Focus and Direction

One final truth about focus: you always move toward what you fix your eyes on. If you fix your gaze on failure, you'll move toward fear. If you fix it on the past, you'll move toward paralysis. But if you fix your eyes on values and purpose, you'll move toward impact.

Focusing forward isn't about ignoring reality, it's about intentionally choosing your direction.

Focusing Forward: Living and Leading with Values

Values as a Compass

If forward is the direction of impact, then values are the compass that keeps us from wandering in circles.

Think of values as the inner "true north" that guides decisions, big and small. Without them, we drift. With them, even in storms, we stay oriented.

What Are Core Values?

Values are not just nice words you hang on a wall or post in a mission statement. They are the deeply held beliefs about what matters most in life. They are the non-negotiables, the principles that remain steady no matter how circumstances shift.

Values are different than ethics and integrity. This is something people confuse all the time. Think of ethics, that is something you either have, or you don't have. It is the same with integrity, you either have integrity, or you don't. Values are different. Everyone of us can value different things. There are no "wrong" values. And our values can change over the course of our life. What you valued when you were 25 may not be the same thing you value at 35 or 55.

For some, it might be integrity, family, service, growth, compassion, or courage. The specific list looks different for each person, but the power comes in being clear on them.

Clarity matters because the world is noisy. Every day, we're bombarded with choices, opportunities, distractions, and demands. Without values, we chase whatever looks shiny in the moment. With values, we pause, measure, and choose with confidence.

Have you ever taken the time to really think about what you really value? Here are some common values people have. Using the list to get you started, I recommend taking some time to identify what your top three to five values are. What are the ones that mean the most to you?

- **Achievement** — Places importance on the fulfillment of activities, goals, tasks, or work.

- **Adventure** — Seeks out and/or participates in exciting events that involve uncertainty.

- **Autonomy** — places importance on freedom, independence, and individual discretion.

- **Challenges** — things or situations that test a person's thoughts or abilities.

- **Change** — a shift from one state, or phase to another.

- **Community** — a group of people with a common background or characteristic or with shared interest.

- **Competence** — ability to solve problems, demonstrate mastery.

- **Competition** — comparison of self, team, or organization against oneself or another.

- **Cooperation** — placing importance on working together to achieve results; go along with a role.

- **Creativity** — placing importance on imagination, inspiration, and inventiveness.

- **Decisiveness** — the ability to make decisions firmly, clearly, conclusively and in a timely manner.

- **Diversity** — appreciates and respects individual differences.

- **Ecology/Environment** — awareness of natural resources.

- **Education** — places importance on learning and education.

- **Ethics** — valuing moral standards.

- **Excellence** — Pursuit of the highest level of optimal performance.

- **Excitement** — Things that engage attention and/or emotion, in a lively, stimulating way.

- **Fairness** — placing importance in justice, equality, and decency.

- **Fame** — Recognition by others, desires to be well known.

- **Family** — Connection to immediate or extended relations.

- **Flexibility** — the ability to adapt to different environments, situations, or change.

- **Freedom** — without obligation.

- **Happiness** — Feelings of contentment, satisfaction, and/or fulfillment.

Once you have identified your values spend some time with them. Write them on a post it note and put them on your mirror or someplace you can look at them. Give yourself some time to connect with them, marinate in them, and decide what they really mean to you. One thing I have discovered is what we originally think we value may not necessarily be the ones that really stick with us and remember values can change over time.

The next step is, are you "living" your values? I say this with so much love, because it is not as easy as one might think. This means, if I observe your behavior for a week would I be able to tell what your values are?

I have always said, one of my values is family. I know, shocking! It is one of the most popular values people claim. I don't have any children of my own, the biggest regret of my life for sure, but I digress. I do have an amazing, wonderful husband and 6 perfect nieces! I adore my nieces so much and being the best Aunt Juju is my most important goal in life. If you ask me about them I am ready to bust out the pictures and tell the stories, I mean, I have no doubt you would agree that they are absolutely adorable! Definitely one of my core values.

I had been traveling quite a bit for work, as usual. I was going to be on the road all week not getting home until Friday night. And I was leaving for my next trip on Sunday. So, I had one day at home to see my husband, unpack, repack, prep, and do all the things. On Tuesday my sister sends me a text message asking me if I want to come over on Saturday and spend a couple of hours with my two youngest nieces. My sister and her wife had someplace they needed to be, and it would help them out if I could watch the littles for a couple of hours. Then she added that my nieces would love to see me! True confessions, my first response was...arghhhh. I am so embarrassed to say that, but it is true. I was selfishly, just thinking about myself. Then a little voice in my head said, what do you really value? And I realized it was my nieces. If that meant that I needed to stay up a little later Saturday or get up a little earlier on Sunday to get things done, then that is what I needed to do. Then I could prioritize my nieces and that is in line with my core values.

The lesson that I was reminded of that day was the importance of living your values. If you say you value honesty, for example, are you living a life that's honest? If that clerk at the store accidentally gives you too much change, do you tell them? If you say you value your faith or religion and never go to church, are you living your values? You get the idea. It is one thing to SAY that value something, but are you living it? When we are clear on our values then decisions we make every day become easier. Like the decision to spend those few hours with my nieces was a no brainer when I used my values in the decision process.

Values cut deeper than the surface. They help us ask questions like what do I stand for, what do I refuse to compromise on, and when pressure comes, what stays steady?

When we are clear on our values, our values endure and focusing forward becomes easier.

Decision-Making with Values

Every day, you and I are shaping the future, not through one massive choice, but through hundreds of small ones. Each decision is like a brushstroke, and over time, those strokes create the portrait of your life and the impact you make.

So how do we make decisions that align with our values and keep us focused forward?

Slow Down to Speed Up

One of the biggest mistakes in decision-making is rushing. We often make choices out of impulse, fear, or pressure. Values invite us to slow down. They give us permission to pause, reflect, and ask: What's the wise thing to do here? What aligns with who I want to be?

Slowing down may feel inefficient, but in the long run, it speeds us up—because we avoid costly detours caused by poor, reactive choices.

Have a Practical Framework

Here's a simple process for values-based decision-making:

- **Clarify your values**. Write them down. Keep them visible. Don't assume you'll "just know."

- **Ask the alignment question**. Does this option reflect my core values or contradict them?

- **Consider the ripple effect**. Who will be impacted by this decision? Will it build trust, or erode it?

- **Choose forward**. When in doubt, pick the option that moves you closer to your future vision, not back toward your past fears.

This framework keeps us grounded and forward-facing at the same time.

How does this show up in the real world? It happens more often than most of us realize. It can happen at work, maybe you're offered a promotion that comes with prestige but requires you to sacrifice evenings with your kids. If family is your core value, then the choice is simple, you may say no, even if it surprises others.

As a leader, this can feel even more frustrating. Maybe you face pressure to cut corners in order to meet short-term results. But if your value is excellence, you commit to quality, knowing the long-term trust it builds is worth more than a quick win.

Clarity of values anchor us when circumstances pull in multiple directions.

When you are consistent it gets even better. When we make decisions based on values, people begin to see us as trustworthy and dependable. They know what we stand for. They don't have to guess whether we'll bend under pressure.

This consistency builds credibility, and credibility multiplies impact. In fact, one of the greatest ways to make a difference in the lives of others is simply to live in such alignment with your values that others find courage to live by theirs.

Modern life bombards us with endless choices, and decision fatigue is real. But values simplify. Instead of a thousand competing options, you're left with one guiding question: Does this align with who I want to be?

That clarity is powerful. It removes hesitation, reduces regret, and multiplies impact.

Focusing Forward Requires Vision.

Focusing forward isn't simply about moving, it's about moving with direction. And that direction comes from vision.

Vision is the picture of the future that pulls you forward. Without it, life becomes a series of disconnected choices. With it, every step gains purpose.

It's one thing to dream about tomorrow; it's another to walk toward it. Vision always calls us out of comfort zones. It asks us to trade the certainty of the past for the possibility of the future.

Some people think that vision can sound lofty, that it's all about vision boards with pictures cut out of magazines, or on whiteboards, or journal pages. Personally, I am not a fan. I believe vision is meant to live in your daily choices.

A couple of thoughts on how to make vision a part of your life. First, take time to imagine the life you want to create, not just for yourself, but for the people around you. Instead, ask yourself questions like what kind of impact do I want to leave in my family, my work, my community? Or what will people say changed because I lived with values and vision?

Write this down. Let it become the North Star that pulls your focus forward. No magazine pictures required!

Once you've defined the picture, reverse-engineer it. If your vision is to be a leader who empowers others, what does that mean for how you lead a meeting today? If your vision is to raise children who know they're deeply loved, what does that mean for how you show up at the dinner table tonight? How are you living that vision? Your big vision and consequently the impact you leave is reached through consistent small steps. Every choice either carries you closer to the picture or away from it.

Then continue to focus forward. That is the point of the chapter, isn't it? Vision dies when we keep glancing backward. Just like a runner loses speed if they constantly look over their shoulder, you lose momentum when your gaze is locked on yesterday. Instead, learn to ask yourself what's ahead of me that needs my focus?

The past is a classroom, not a destination. The future is where your impact lives.

The Company You Keep Matters.

The people around you will either feed your vision or drain it. Build a circle of vision-builders, those who remind you of where you're going, encourage your values, and challenge you to stay focused when distractions arise. Impact multiplies in community. Your vision is bigger than you, and you'll need others to help carry it forward.

At the end of the day, forward focus is not about perfection—it's about impact.

Your impact doesn't happen by accident; it's the fruit of a vision lived out with consistency. When you live with clear values and a future-focused vision, your choices ripple beyond your own life. They touch your children, your colleagues, your neighbors, and even people you may never meet.

Your impact will not be defined by what you avoided, but by the vision you pursued.

When you focus forward, anchored in vision, something remarkable happens:

- Your courage sparks courage in others.
- Your resilience strengthens someone else's resolve.
- Your forgiveness frees others to release their own pain.
- Your clarity invites others to pursue their vision with boldness.

This is impact—living in such a way that your forward focus creates forward focus in those around you.

Every day presents a choice: to dwell on what has been or to invest in what could be. Your vision will not come alive by looking behind. It will only grow when you choose, again and again, to put your focus forward.

Ask yourself daily: Am I making choices that build the future I want, or am I replaying the past I cannot change?

So, my invitation to you is simple.

Lift your eyes from the rearview mirror.

Define the vision that inspires you.

Anchor yourself in the values that keep you steady.

Step courageously, one small choice at a time, toward the future.

Because your life is not just about today, it's about the future you are creating, the impact you are leaving, and the impact you are making in the lives around you.

Forward focus is not simply about where you are going. It's about who you are becoming and the impact you create along the way.

The truth is, the world doesn't just need more people who dwell on the past. The world needs people of vision, people who can see what's possible, live by their values, and walk forward with courage.

So, focus forward. Let vision pull you. Let values guide you. And let your impact echo far beyond your own life.

Because your greatest impact is not behind you. It's ahead. And the future is waiting for you to step into it.

So, who are you becoming?

Chapter 4

Visible, Vulnerable, & Worth It

(Playing small is exhausting and wildly overrated)

Since you have made it this far into the book, I am assuming making an impact is your jam! And my goal is to give you both tangible skills you can take and apply immediately as well as a little mindset shift to help you take action. If you checked out the table of contents you saw chapters on communication, emotional intelligence, prioritizing and productivity, dealing with change, building resilience and sharpening focus. Those are all skill-based ideas.

However, for the skills to work for you, your mindset must be in the right space too. And let's get real. This is where most people fail.

What ties all of them together, the mind and the action, and what studies consistently show is a struggle for people as they work to level up, achieve more, be more, do more, and make more of an impact may surprise you.

The fear of visibility is the problem. Not failure. Visibility.

People SAY they are afraid of failure, but most of the time what they are actually afraid of are things like being seen, being judged, disappointing people, criticism, rejection, success changing our relationships, outgrowing old identities, standing out, owning their voice, and even fully stepping into leadership. THAT is the hidden barrier.

People do not stay stuck because they lack talent.

They stay stuck because visibility feels vulnerable. And no one likes to feel vulnerable. I promise you, I have struggled with this my entire life. I never want to feel weak or appear to be weak, so I have spent many years being quiet. And consequently, quietly unheard. For a professional speaker, being unheard seems crazy but remember, I have done a lot of presentations, but it took me a long time to be authentic.

Not that I wasn't told I should be more vulnerable. My sister, who is my hero, is so good at just laying it out there. She tells her story, complete with all the challenges, fears, mistakes, everything, she lets everyone in. That never felt safe for me. I always wanted to keep my past, in the past. Because well, it wasn't always pretty or something I was proud of. I wanted it to stay hidden.

Fear of visibility.

I wasn't really afraid I would fail or afraid I would succeed; I was afraid I would be seen. And then judged. And I knew that was going to hurt.

In the first chapter of this book, I briefly shared my story of being a victim of domestic violence. And when I wrote that chapter, it was the first time I had ever confessed it so publicly. Before that there were less than a handful of people on the planet that knew about that so writing it down seemed too overwhelming.

But I did it. And guess what? As soon as I did it, I felt better. I felt a weight lift off my shoulders and I felt somehow freer. My sister told me this would happen, but up until then, I really didn't want to take the chance she was wrong.

Then shortly after writing it down, I said it out loud. In front of an audience of 1000 people. I wasn't originally planning to share it. I had my keynote written and was ready to go. Sitting in my hotel room the night before I was reviewing my presentation as I always do. And in that moment, I thought this would fit in this piece pretty perfectly. It would be a great real-life example for the point I was planning on making. But...was I ready? So, I wrote a few notes about it and decided I would decide on stage in the morning! If it came out of my mouth so, be it, if not that's fine too.

The next morning, I am standing on stage with over 1000 people staring at me... and the story just came out. I said it. Out loud. In front of 1000 people. My first thought was, Holy crap, what have I done? You can't put the toothpaste back in the tube. It was out there now. And I was terrified. But the faces in the crowd, the ones I could see anyway, (it was a big stage with a lot of lights) they didn't look disgusted, or judgmental at all. They looked "seen." Like they just felt they get lighter and freer. I wasn't sure what was happening, but it seemed to be OK.

I got a standing ovation after my keynote, which always makes me want to cry. But something else happened, feedback I had never heard before. I had so many women come up to me afterward and thank me. Thank me for my honesty, one woman actually said the words "Thank you for being so vulnerable. I had a similar situation, and you really made me feel better. There is hope!" Another told me a story about her daughter, and one about her cousin. And they just kept coming. What I learned was that by me being vulnerable it somehow made it OK for others to do the same.

If we want to make a bigger impact in our lives and on the lives of those around us, we must start by being authentic. When you are authentic you are relatable. And people connect with people that are relatable.

Does this potentially open you up to some haters? Sure, I suppose it does. But remember, most of that happens behind the curtain of social media not in personal interactions. Don't listen to the haters— they don't have your best interest at heart anyway. You got to be like Teflon, Baby! Nothing sticks!

Let me give you a little truth bomb. Maybe I can lovingly kick you in the mindset here, because I am about to preach. You need to know this, our ability to level up and change our lives and our impact are going to require you to take a hard look in the mirror. And like Michael Jackson says "It starts with the man in the mirror."

We say we want to do something different, make an impact, and change the world even! But it starts with the person in the mirror.

There is a great old wives' tale, maybe you have heard it. I shared it on our podcast, "Breakthrough with Mallory and Julie" (You can listen anywhere you get your podcasts! Shameless plug complete.) The story is about a professor at a high school that brought in a Buddhist Monk to speak to his class about enlightenment. The Monk walked slowly into the classroom, turned his back to the class, picked up a piece of chalk and started to write on the chalkboard. He simply wrote, "You want to change the world, but you won't even help your Mom with the dishes." Bam. That's a mic drop moment!

Think about that. Changing the world seems big and unattainable so it's easy to do nothing. But it isn't always the big things that make a difference. We tend to fall into the trap of the dichotomy of two choices. It's either all or it's nothing. We change the world or we throw our hands up and say nothing we can do will ever matter.

It is not everything or nothing. The answer is something.

Its small steps. What CAN you do? Maybe it starts with doing the dishes. The key is you have to be an active participant in your own life. When you do nothing, nothing changes. But even small changes create a ripple effect that can become life changing.

I use a lot of examples about losing weight, exercise, healthy lifestyle and all that crap because it is an ever present part of my life. I have been on every diet known to man over the years some of them more than once. I am pretty sure I have lost and gained back the exact same 40 pounds multiple times. I did however recently make a bigger change. Well, that's not true. I made some small changes and made them consistently. I have now lost 80 pounds, as of writing this with a lot more to go. So don't look at me too closely if you see me in person. The point is it wasn't one big giant thing I did. I didn't go to the gym once and then expect to be down 3 dress sizes the next day. It was small consistent steps. You don't have to do big things; you can do small things with great care and consistency.

There is an interesting old book out there by Alvin Toffler titled "Future Shock." It came out in the 1970's so it's an older book. But in it, Toffler makes this interesting prediction. He says that the illiterate on the 21st Century will not be people that can't read or write. The illiterate people will be the people that can't "Learn—unlearn—and Re-learn." Let that soak in for a minute. That is powerful. And true.

Think about all the things you have learned in your lifetime. Now think about all things you have learned in your lifetime that are irrelevant or out of date. We learn things only to then not need that skill again. I remember my first Blackberry phone. And rest assured, I am not an early adopter, so I didn't have one right away. I remember all the time I spent trying to learn how to use it, just how to text on it took some time! I haven't used a Blackberry in years, so I had to unlearn it. And relearn with my iPhone. And don't get me started with how I reacted when they took away my home button! Maybe some of you remember Ask Jeeves. Google's grandpa! Again, we learn—unlearn—and re-learn all the time. And we haven't even discussed the power of AI and all the learning we are doing there.

Our willingness to learn—unlearn—and re-learn will make us unstoppable. Talk about making an impact. What skills do you need? What skill would you need to give you the advantage in your field? What would make you better? Identify them. Then DO them. I have been speaking professionally for, what seems like forever. I am very grateful! But I have been doing this so long that when I started in the business, we didn't use laptops and PowerPoint. We used an overhead projector and transparencies! Think 4th grade math class! Could you imagine if you came to a conference and the speaker busted out an old overhead projector like you were in grade school again what you would think? You probably wouldn't have a lot of faith in the content you were listening to either.

The truth bombs just keep coming. Adapt or die. What got you where you are, the skills you originally brought to the table, are probably not the same skills that you are going to need to level up now.

But after I hit you with the hard truth, now I will lovingly nudge you in the mindset. The good news is, you have way more skills within you that you haven't come close to tapping into yet. And more importantly, you can learn anything! As Marie Forleo says, "everything is figure out able!" And remember, it's not everything or nothing. It's something. What small step can you take?

Taking action can feel vulnerable and risky, but I think we covered that for now. We will dig deeper on the whole "taking a risk" part in the last chapter. (So, keep reading!)

And when the road gets long or seems too hard to handle or success—or even just relief— feels out of reach. When the overwhelm starts to creep in, always keep this in the back of your mind, the hardest thing that has ever happened to you is the hardest thing that has ever happened to you. And that hard thing doesn't diminish because someone else experienced something worse. Hardship isn't a competition. And that's great news. Because that means the hardest thing you have ever been through, you survived! And you will survive this too. And don't let other people try to compare their despair. People like that are the worst. You know the ones I mean. The "one-uppers?" The people that no matter what you have done they have done it better, faster, first or had it harder or worse. Ignore them, they suck. Don't let them cramp your jam.

If our goal for this chapter is to overcome the fear of visibility, what are some ways this might show up in our lives so we can work to change our behavior? Remember, as James Clear, the author of Atomic Habits says, "Every action you take is a vote for the type of person you wish to become."

What kind of person do you want to become? I wanted to become someone who cared about living a healthier lifestyle. So, I made small decisions in the direction every day. It becomes like a feedback loop. When you use the good behavior it reminds you what kind of person you are, so you do more of that behavior. However way too often, you keep asking for confidence while hiding from every opportunity that could build it. Time to build it!

Real-life examples

What are some of the most common times people fear visibility and then shrink when instead they should speak?

Staying quiet in meetings. This is so common. Maybe you have been there. When you have something to say, to contribute, or hell, you could just plain solve the problem, if you could get a word in edgewise! Or if someone would bother to ask you! Stop waiting to be saved princess, no one is coming to save you, you have to save yourself. If you have something to say, just say it! The worst thing that happens is you are wrong, in which case you can say, "Thank you for clarifying, I am so glad I spoke up!"

Not applying for jobs. This is an interesting statistic, I wish I could remember exactly where it came from but, in general it boils down to this. When applying for a job, a woman will read the job description and apply for the position only if, in her head she has at least 90-95% of the stated job skills already mastered to think she is qualified. For men, they only think they need 55-60% of the stated skills, citing that they can learn whatever they don't already know. What? That is wild to me. Women don't apply for jobs because they disqualify themselves. Stop that! Can you learn the skills? Do you bring other skills to the table? Don't limit yourself, explore all the options. Remember the goal is to stay visible and not shrink.

Refusing opportunities. This is the same basic problem; we refuse because we unqualified ourselves! You are capable of so much more. Trust yourself.

Here are a few more in rapid fire to watch for:

- Downplaying accomplishments or hiding talents. Be willing to share your value. You must own it. I say name it and claim it! Some of y'all are overqualified for the life you're currently tolerating, so own those good things.

- Staying in unhealthy situations. You are strong enough to move on. If I can do it, you can do it. You deserve more. And this can be relationships, friends, and jobs!

- Not writing the book. This one might just be me. But here we are! So, just do it!

- Not speaking up. Say what you mean and mean what you say.

- Shrinking personality. Your personality should not shrink based on who is in the room. Be authentic. Your comfort zone may have excellent snacks but it definitely has terrible growth potential.

- Apologizing constantly. This is such an annoying trait. If you make a mistake, own it and apologize. ONCE. If you didn't make a mistake, then you don't need to apologize. Here is a self-test to see if this is something you might want to pay attention to. If you are, let's say, grocery shopping at the Publix or The Piggly Wiggly, or wherever you prefer to get your eats. and you are pushing your buggy down the aisle, and someone has their buggy parked across the aisle blocking your way.

What do you say?

"I'm sorry, could I get by?" or "Excuse me, may I get by?" You weren't blocking the aisle; they were. So, you know which one is more appropriate.

Waiting for permission. The last one, and I can't stress this enough, stop waiting for permission. Step up and go for it. Making an impact rarely requires permission. Because really, at this point, some people are not protecting their peace—they are avoiding their purpose. So stop it.

The deeper emotional layer

I appreciate that for many of us we were conditioned to stay quiet. We may have learned very early that it was safer that way. Definitely safer than being visible anyway. It can come from lots of different places for people. It could be you were a child of the generation that was told they should be seen but not heard. Maybe you grew up in a volatile household where staying invisible and quiet was required for sheer safety. Maybe you grew up and were told that it's not ladylike to speak up too loudly or too much. Your job was to just sit there and be pretty.

There are as many deep emotional scars around this idea as there are people that feel it. First of all, you need to know that it's OK if that is your life experience. It's OK that it happened, it's NOT OK to stay there.

Now is the time to change that mindset. For yourself and for the younger ones that look up to you! Would you want your child to feel that way? If your answer is no, but you still DO it. Which lesson do you think they will learn?

And honestly? I think this concept is more powerful than any generic motivation poster or concept you may hear. Because it gets to the real issue:

People are not lacking potential.

They are lacking permission to fully show up.

Because impact requires visibility.

You cannot change rooms while hiding in corners.

So don’t let them put Baby in the corner!

Chapter 5

If Everything Matters, Nothing Does

(Priorities, boundaries, and why burnout is not a badge of honor)

If there is one topic that can make even the most competent, capable, hard-working people feel a little exposed, it is this one. Time management. Productivity. Priorities. Call it what you want, but the minute the conversation starts, most people have the same reaction. They straighten up, laugh a little nervously, and think, Well, this should be interesting, because I am pretty sure I am doing at least three things wrong before breakfast.

I understand that reaction, and honestly, I think it is fair. This is one of those subjects that sounds simple until you actually try to live it. Most of us know, at least in theory, that we should be more focused, more organized, and more intentional. We know we should not waste time. We know we should prioritize. We know we should not let every email, interruption, and random request hijack our day. And yet, somehow, all of that good common sense can disappear by 9:17 a.m. when our phone rings, our inbox lights up, somebody drops by "for just a second," and the one thing we truly needed to get done gets pushed to the side yet again.

That is why I always start this conversation with what I call my disclaimer and my reality check. If we are going to talk honestly about productivity and prioritizing, we need a little truth right up front.

My disclaimer is this: I am not here to teach you how to be busy.

That may sound strange at first because, for a lot of people, busy feels like the goal. Busy feels productive. Busy sounds important. Busy looks impressive from the outside. But busy does not equal results. It just does not. We all know people who are ridiculously busy. They are the ones who always seem to be in motion. They are hurrying, talking, answering, reacting, and sighing dramatically as they tell you how busy they are. They stay in a constant swirl of activity. And yet, when you look closely, they are not necessarily accomplishing much of real value. They are moving, but not moving the needle.

What makes that moment so frustrating is that it doesn't feel like you wasted your day. It feels like you gave everything you had to it. You were responsive. You were helpful. You showed up. You handled what came your way. And yet, the one thing you needed to move forward is still sitting there, untouched, quietly waiting for "when you have time."

That disconnect is where people start to question themselves. Am I just not disciplined enough? Am I not organized enough? Why does it feel like I'm working so hard but not getting anywhere?

But the issue is not your effort. The issue is direction.

If you pour all of your energy into the wrong things, you can end the day completely drained and still feel like you are standing in the exact same place you started.

And that is one of the fastest ways to lose confidence in yourself.

That distinction matters, especially if your bigger goal is not just to survive your day but to make an impact with your life. You cannot create a life of meaning by being endlessly active. You create a life of meaning by being intentional. That is true in your work, in your leadership, in your relationships, and in the way you choose to spend your energy. Being busy may make you feel needed. It may even make you look important. But results come from doing the right things, not from doing all the things.

Then comes the reality check. Is it realistic to think that you can read a chapter like this, pick up a few ideas, and never struggle with productivity or time management again? Of course not. That is not how life works. You are not going to finish this chapter and suddenly become a magical productivity unicorn who can complete thirty-eight hours of work in an eight-hour day while also answering every email, color-coding every file, meal-prepping for the week, and becoming a better version of yourself by lunchtime.

That is not realistic. But here is what is realistic. It is realistic to believe that if you become more intentional, if you learn to identify where your time is going, and if you begin to make better choices with greater consistency, you can absolutely improve. You can save time. You can reduce stress. You can stop wasting so much energy on the wrong things. And maybe most importantly, you can stop feeling so stuck.

I often tell audiences that if we can save just an hour a day, that matters. An hour a day is meaningful. But the lesson hidden inside that idea is even more important. Most people do not have a free hour sitting around in the middle of their day just waiting to be found. There is no mysterious block of unused time hanging out behind your computer screen. We do not usually find time in big, dramatic chunks. We find it in small pieces, in smarter choices, in better boundaries, in fewer distractions, and in the discipline to stop doing things that make us feel productive without actually producing anything meaningful.

That is why I believe time management is really a misleading phrase. We say time management because that is the language everybody recognizes, but the truth is, there is no such thing as managing time. Time does not care what you do. It just keeps moving. Nobody gets more of it than anyone else. You cannot save it for tomorrow. You cannot negotiate for more of it. You cannot put in a request and ask life to give you a little extra on Tuesday because Monday was chaotic.

What you can manage is yourself.

You can manage your focus. You can manage your behavior. You can manage your priorities. You can manage your habits, your reactions, your boundaries, your choices, and your willingness to do what matters instead of what is easiest. And that is where the conversation gets powerful, because the moment you realize this is really about self-management, not time-management, the power comes back to you.

That matters in a book about impact, because a lot of people say they want to do more, be more, and have more, but what they really mean is that they want their life to matter. They want to contribute something meaningful. They want to feel effective instead of scattered. They want to stop ending every day exhausted and vaguely disappointed. They want to know they are making a difference in their own life and in the lives of the people around them. But you cannot do that if all your energy is being poured into reacting. You cannot create impact if you are spending your whole life putting out fires and calling it progress.

So let me give you the working definition that shapes everything that follows. Time management is about doing the right things in the right order. That is it. It is not about getting it all done. It is not about becoming a machine. It is not about seeing how many items you can cram into a day before you collapse on the couch and stare blankly at the ceiling. It is about doing the right things in the right order.

Once you understand that, a lot of your frustration starts to make more sense.

Over the years, I have noticed that while people experience productivity challenges in all kinds of different ways, there are four destructive time management styles that show up again and again. They are not the only problems people have, but they are common, and they are sneaky, because they often masquerade as competence. I call them the Busy Bee, the Fire Chief, the Procrastinator, and the Superhero.

Let us start with the Busy Bee, because this one fools a lot of people. On the surface, being busy sounds good. It sounds responsible. It sounds like a hard worker. But the problem with the Busy Bee is that this person is active without being effective. They work on this for a little bit, then that for a little bit, then they get pulled into something else, then they circle back halfway, then someone stops by and now they are helping with that. They are constantly moving, but they are not completing. I always think of the Busy Bee as the person who finishes half of everything. They are working on enough tasks to feel overwhelmed, but not following through enough to feel accomplished.

Everybody knows this feeling. You get to the end of the day and you cannot really point to anything meaningful you completed. You touched everything. You handled a little bit of this and a little bit of that. You were absolutely busy. But when it comes time to cross something off your list, there is nothing satisfying there. You have lived in fragments. And fragments are exhausting.

Then there is the Fire Chief. In real life, I love a fireman. My husband is a retired fireman, so I have nothing but affection for firefighters. But as a time management style, the Fire Chief can be a problem. This is the person who spends the whole day putting out fires. Every issue is a crisis. Every interruption demands immediate attention. Every incoming request gets handled as if it belongs at the top of the pile. The result is that the Fire Chief lives in reaction mode. There is no space for planning, prevention, or thoughtful work because all day is spent responding.

One of the most important questions I ask people who identify with this style is this: whose fires are you putting out? Because very often, the Fire Chief is not even spending the day solving their own highest priorities. They are solving everyone else's. They are putting out other people's fires while their own important work sits there waiting. They are needed, yes. They are responsive, yes. They may even be admired for how quickly they jump in. But the cost is that they never actually move their own priorities forward.

I had a workshop moment that captured this so perfectly that I still laugh when I think about it. I was doing a full-day session on productivity, and there was a woman sitting in the back of the room who had not said a word all day. She looked engaged. She was making eye contact and taking notes, but she did not speak. Near the end of the session, I mentioned interruptions, and suddenly her hand shot up. When I called on her, she said, with great passion, that interruptions were her problem. Her phone never stopped ringing. If her phone would just stop ringing, she could finally get her work done. The room nodded with sympathy because, honestly, who has not felt that? I looked at her and said, "Tell me what you do." With a straight face, she said, "I'm the receptionist."

I could not help her.

Because if you are the receptionist, the phone ringing is not an interruption to your work. It is your work.

The room burst out laughing, and even she laughed once she heard herself say it. But that moment made a valuable point. Not everything that feels like an interruption is bad. Some things are built into your role. Some interruptions are part of the value you create. The problem is not that interruptions exist. The problem is that we do not distinguish between the interruptions that are part of our job and the ones we allow to derail us unnecessarily.

Then comes the Procrastinator, and let us be honest, this is the one that nobody wants to admit to while also secretly recognizing themselves in every description. The challenge with procrastination is not just that it delays work. It is that it creates false urgency. When you put things off, especially things that are important, they do not disappear. They simply move closer to a deadline. Then suddenly what could have been handled steadily over time becomes urgent, stressful, and messy.

People love to say they work better under pressure. I understand why they say it. Pressure creates adrenaline, and adrenaline can make you feel sharp. But most of the time, that sentence is not really true. People do not usually work better under pressure. They just waited until pressure showed up. That is not a productivity system. That is a coping mechanism.

Finally, there is the Superhero. This one can look noble on the surface because it often comes from genuinely good intentions. Superheroes want to help. They care. They want to support the team. They want to save the day. But whether it comes from kindness or from a need to control everything, the end result is often the same: they take on too much. They become the person everyone depends on. They swoop in, solve, fix, rescue, and carry. And then they are shocked to discover they are overwhelmed, resentful, and exhausted.

The hardest truth about the Superhero is that you teach people how to treat you. If you always say yes, people will keep bringing you things. If you always save the day, people will start to expect it. If you keep proving that you will pick up the slack, take on the extra load, and manage things no one else wants to handle, people will assume that is what you do. Then one day, you look around and wonder why you are drowning.

The answer is not because you are weak. It is because the pattern was never interrupted.

What is interesting about these four styles is that they are connected. They do not exist in isolation. In fact, they often create a cycle. The Fire Chief spends the day putting out fires. That constant reactivity turns them into the Busy Bee, darting from thing to thing. Because they spend all day being busy in reaction mode, they procrastinate the meaningful work they should be doing. Then when that work becomes urgent, they try to save it all as the Superhero. And around and around they go.

If that sounds familiar, it is because it is familiar. This is what a lot of people are living. Not because they are irresponsible, but because systems create behavior, and bad systems create bad patterns.

That is why getting unstuck requires more than good intentions. It requires new choices.

Chapter 6

You Make Me So Mad!

(Emotional intelligence for the rest of us)

Making an impact in your life isn't about one big, bold moment, it's about how you show up in the small ones, especially the hard ones. It's in the conversations where you're frustrated, the moments where you're triggered, and the split-second decisions where you can either react... or respond. That's where emotional intelligence and emotional control come together, and that's where real agency begins. Because the truth is, if you don't take control of your emotions, they will take control of you—and that will shape your outcomes whether you intend it to or not. Learning to manage your emotions doesn't make you less human; it makes you more intentional. And when you become intentional about how you think, speak, and respond, you stop living on autopilot and start actively creating the impact—and the life—you actually want.

I have been teaching developing your emotional intelligence for years. My approach has always been more "real world" less "textbook." No one wants to analytically understand emotional intelligence without the ability to practice it in real life. So that is what I am going to give you in this chapter. My version of emotional intelligence, so buckle up buttercup!

When I talk about developing your emotional intelligence and managing your emotions in the workplace in a live event, I always do this exercise. And I know we can't do the same exact exercise, but I want to do a version of it, sort of a virtual exercise with you instead. I want to give you an emotional connection to this idea as we dive in. So, just play along with me here.

Put yourself in a meeting space, picture yourself in a big conference room. There's a bunch of tables. You're sitting there. Groups of people. And I want you to visualize what happens here. I tell everyone in the room, "Okay, everyone, we're going to do a group exercise. You're going to work with the people around you. But I'll tell you what. Boy, y'all look hungry. You probably need a snack. You need a little candy, a little sugar rush."

I pull out big bags of candy and I pass the bags of candy around the room. While I tell everyone to take a piece of candy and pass the bag. Everyone gets a piece of candy, take a piece of candy, and pass the bag. While I have everyone passing the bag and I tell them, grab a piece of candy, you can eat it now, that's fine. It's your candy. Or you can wait. You may get more later if you wait. Just pass the bag. Now they're passing the bags.

While they do that, I say, "Okay, so here's your exercise." Super simple. I want you all to identify what is America's best-selling candy brand. So, they're passing the candy and they're evaluating this question.

Now, I want the audience to talk to me about what happened in this exercise. I pose the question, "What percentage of the people in an average audience would you say ate their candy?" I get a crazy array of responses. People will guess anywhere from 20% to 90%.

Now, true confessions, this is not a scientific poll. This is just what I've observed with my audiences. I have done this training over the years. But I'll tell you about 50% of my audience will generally eat the candy. The next question obviously becomes, why did they choose to eat it or why did they not eat the candy? What made them choose one or the other? People will say, "Well, because it's there, because I was hungry, because I can't turn down Reese's peanut butter cup, I don't like chocolate." (I never understood those people. Who doesn't like chocolate?!) I get all kinds of answers. However, very few people will say, "Well, because you told me that if I don't eat it, I might get more later." That might be the idea. Now, I promise you I say it every time, but y'all would be amazed at how many people don't hear that part of what I said. Now, I do all of this to introduce the marshmallow test.

If you're not familiar with it, this is one of my favorite things. The marshmallow test was a study that was done back in the 1960s. You know those crazy '60s, right? At Stanford University. And what they did was this, they used four year old children for the study. They would have one four year old child, put them in a room with a table, a chair, and one big marshmallow, and they would tell the child, "This is your marshmallow. You can eat the marshmallow. I'm going to go run a couple errands. When I come back, if you have not finished your marshmallow, then I will reward you with a second marshmallow." And the facilitator left the room. How many of those kids gobbled up that marshmallow? I know I would have eaten it.

As adults, we understand what's happening. They're measuring delayed gratification. Can you put off the instant gratification of one marshmallow for the delayed gratification of two marshmallows? That's the idea.

What percentage of the kids waited? I was stunned to discover; a full two thirds of the children waited for the second marshmallow. I was impressed.

Part of the reason I find this study so interesting is the 4 year old children that they used were kids of the professors, the teaching assistants, administration from the university.

Which meant they had access to these same children 12 and 14 years down the road when these kids were getting ready to graduate from high school. They talked to their teachers, their parents, they talked to administration, they looked at their records, their test scores, everything. And this is what they discovered.

This is a recap of what they found in the study. And this is directly from a book titled *The EQ Edge*, by Steven J. Stein:

"The kids who had gobbled up a single marshmallow were having one or two problems. As a group, they were less adept at making social contacts, more prone to be stubborn and indecisive. They yielded readily to frustration as well as temptation. Those who had put their gratification on hold and by doing so, doubled their pleasure with a second marshmallow were more successful. They showed more social skills, exhibited superior coping mechanisms, and in general were ahead of the game. This was reflected in their grades. They were, simply put, better students and had scored remarkably better on their SAT test. It sounds incredible, but the ability at age four to wait for a second marshmallow was twice as accurate a predictor of a kid's future SAT score than his or her IQ."

What? How is that possible? Now, I don't know how accurate that study would be if it were done today, but I love this because I do think that understanding emotional intelligence or managing our emotions is in essence delayed gratification.

The other thing about the study that I really love is they used four year old children. That's actually significant because child psychologists tell us as early as age four that our emotional reactions are already starting to set. So that means those habits are being created. When the trigger happens, whatever that trigger is that sets us off, triggers our emotional habits. How we react to that trigger becomes the habit and is already starting to solidify. So, at four years old, where the heck are we learning those emotional reactions to those triggers? Well, from our parents, our teachers, the adults around us. If every day your dad had a bad day at work, he came home and he threw something that becomes normal behavior. We learn it from a very young age from the adults around us.

Four year old toddlers also learn from what works for them. Think about how many times, and I'd be willing to bet every one of us have heard this, when a toddler is having a tantrum, what are we supposed to do? Let them go.

We don't give in, right? Because if we give in, what are we teaching them? We're teaching them that that is a way to get what they want. And I say this with so much love. I have not raised any children of my own. I have amazing nieces, but I don't have any kids of my own, but I feel for you. Those of you that have that four year old, because I've been with you at the Walmart, y'all know what I'm talking about. When they're having that little come apart at the Walmart where they're losing it, "I want that candy." And you're trying so hard to be a good parent! You respond firmly, "No, it'll ruin your dinner." They continue to scream "I want candy!" Finally you just tell them to take the candy because they are making a scene and drawing unwanted attention. I really do feel for you because I've been there. And it's kind of cute when they're four years old at the Walmart. Not nearly as cute when they're 40 years old and they are your coworker! Y'all know exactly what I'm talking about.

If we are creating these habits as early as age 4, it's no wonder why they become habits when we are older. That's why adults say things like, I can't help it. I just cry, I can't help it, I just get mad. I can't help it. I just... whatever. It really feels like you can't help it because it's a habit that you've had for so many years.

Here's the truth though, habits were created over time and habits can be broken. You really do have the ability to reign that back in, to be able to change those reactions. And that's what we're looking at. I always think of, as adults, the way that it should work is this: the trigger happens, the event happens, whatever it is that sets you off, I like to call it being poked. When it happens our brain says bad, very, very bad. As soon as our brain says bad, very, very bad, we start to feel that emotion. And what we as adults have is, what I call an impulse gate. Picture what I mean. It's like a gate in front of your heart. The impulse gate is there and it holds back all of those emotional reactions that you're feeling, all of those reactions that you want to let out, your impulse gate holds it back.

Picture the process-- the trigger happens, the brain says bad, very, very bad, the impulse gate closes, so we can handle the situation appropriately and effectively in the heat of the moment. After we've handled the situation professionally, now we get to go off to our venting place of choice. We get to open our gate and let our emotions flow forth. That's how it's supposed to work, but y'all know the problem. The problem is a lot of people have some messed up gates! Their gates are stuck open, they're stuck in the mud, and they're hanging off a hinge, whatever it is. We have messed up gates. We must make sure that our impulse gates are in place because that's the heart of emotional intelligence. Basically what we're doing is moving things from a reaction to a response.

I believe Dr. Tom Miller explains this better than anyone I've ever known. And I'm kind of dating myself here, but I learned this from Tom Miller on a cassette tape. That's how long ago it was, but that's how good it is because it's really stuck with me. I don't even remember the name of the tape, but I remember what he said. He explains it like this. We are all a horse and a rider. Our horse is our habit. Our horse is our reaction and if you think about it, if a horse gets spooked, what does a horse do? Well, the horse takes off, right? The horse doesn't pause and think about it. It's not like the horse says," Hmm, should I stay or should I go? "Right? The horse just goes! If a horse gets spooked. The horse is out of there. Make no mistake, we need our horse. It's our horse that allows you to react in the good ways. For example, if you put your hand on a hot stove, it's your horse that says, "Argh!! Ouch!!" and pulls your hand away. If we didn't have our horse, you'd put your hand on a hot stove and think, " Hmm, is that burning flesh I smell? Obviously, not good.

We need our horse, but we all also have a rider. Our rider always has the ability to reign in our horse. So, basically what we're doing, is moving things from an instantaneous habitual reaction to a pause and respond. I always think that we're avoiding that Fried Green Tomatoes moment. Do you remember the movie? When Kathy Bates character is looking for the parking spot at the Piggy Wiggly and it's super-hot outside? She's tired and she's waiting, waiting, waiting for the car to pull out. Finally, the car pulls out and then those two young women in a Volkswagen bug pull in and say, "Face it lady, we're younger and faster." And then she ends up hitting the car 25 times or something crazy.

And she says, "Face it, girls. I'm older and have more insurance." I love that! And I think a lot of us when we watch that, we're like, "Yeah, yeah, yeah, because we love it. We can relate. We feel it. "But in reality, we know that's not the best option.

Here's one of my favorite sayings of all time. I heard Rush Limbaugh say it once and it stuck with me. "Sometimes it's better to do good than to feel good." It would feel good to tell them what you think about them, right? It would feel good just to tell them or to send that nasty email. But is it going to do you any good in the long run? We must challenge ourselves to move things from a reaction to a response.

I do want to dispel a myth about understanding emotions, because a lot of us have been told that you should not have emotions at work. There should be no emotions in the workplace. There's no crying in baseball, right? That is ridiculous. We have emotions. We are human. There's no such thing as an emotion-ectopy. You cannot surgically remove emotions. It doesn't work that way. It's not about emotional elimination. This is really important to understand, because the problem is people think that the only way they can be successful. Well, it doesn't work that way. It's not about eliminating emotion. It's about emotional control.

It's about taking back control of your emotion. And some emotion is good emotion! I mean, who doesn't like happy? Who doesn't like joy? Who doesn't love? Everybody loves love.

Some emotion is good emotion. Even the emotions that we would think of as negative emotions are actually a catalyst for action. It's our negative emotions that get us to do stuff, right? We can logically and analytically know we need to do something, but until we are emotionally invested in it, we do not always take action. Let me give you another great saying. I have no idea where it came from but it is genius! "When the pain of change is less than the pain of staying the same, you'll change." Bam. Powerful.

Let that sink in for a second. When the pain of change is less than the pain of staying the same, you'll change. Now, when we say pain, for our purposes, of course, we're not talking about physical pain. We're talking about mental pain, emotional pain. That feeling of meh. I'm just not happy. I'm not really mad or I'm not really awful. I'm just not happy. I'm meh. But the pain of change, holy cow, change is an unknown! We don't know what we're going to get. So, the pain of staying the same, at least it's a known pain. I always use the illustration, maybe you've had this friend that hates their apartment. They say, "I hate my apartment. It's the worst apartment ever. The people that live above me are a family of 22. They're all cloggers. They all play in a band. They play the drums at three in the morning. They move their furniture every night. They take up all the parking spots. It's the worst apartment ever!" When you hear that, you think, whoa, boy, you better move. But there is the pain of change. They respond, "Oh, then I'd have to find a new apartment. I'd have to pay a deposit. I'd have to move my stuff." The known pain may seem better, but we all have a tipping point, don't we? When we hit our limit and say, "That's it. I'm out of here."

Sometimes the tipping point is small, sometimes it's big. My all-time, favorite example, not just for this topic, my favorite example in the history of examples! This story, happened years ago, but I'm holding onto it because I love it so much and it's a perfect example of what we're talking about.

The guy's name is Steven Slater. He was a flight attendant for JetBlue Airlines. He based in New York. So, as the story happens, he's working a flight heading into New York and apparently, he had some issues with some difficult passengers. As they're pulling into New York, y'all just imagine this... (It makes me want to fly jet blue. I wish I'd have been on this plane!) As you're pulling in, he gets on the PA system and cusses out the passengers! Could y'all imagine being on that plane, you'd be looking at the person next to you like, "Is he talking to us?" Then he grabs two beers, which is my favorite part of the story, takes his two beers, and opens the door, which releases the emergency evacuation slide with his two beers, slides down the slide, and walks to the employee parking lot and drives himself home.

I'm pretty sure it was about the time he was cracking open the second beer, the SWAT team showed up to arrest him. Could you imagine being on that flight? I would've so loved to have seen that complete come apart happen in real time! And I know people are think, "Oh, but your flight would be delayed, and it would be awful." I think, "I know, but how fun to watch!" And here's the deal. Think about it. Do you think that that was his first bad day on the job? Do you think that was his first difficult passenger? No. I think he had a little pent up aggression. I don't think he was processing his emotions effectively. And I stress that. I really do stress that idea of processing. I use the word process by design because that's exactly what has to happen. We process our emotions, and he definitely was not processing his emotions effectively.

When we talk about emotional intelligence, there are four basic components that make up a more technical or textbook definition of emotional intelligence.

First, self-awareness. That means you have to be aware you have feelings. Second, you must have self-management. That means you have the ability or process to manage those emotions effectively. We must have our impulse gate in place to reign in your horse, so that you process those emotions effectively.

The third component of emotional intelligence is social awareness. In a nutshell, that means we have to understand that other people have their own emotions too. And guess what? They're not all the same. Everyone can feel differently. Maybe you can remember a time when someone is having a total come apart or is totally upset about something and you think, that it is ridiculous?

You're looking at them thinking, really? This is why you're upset? And of course, they are being very dramatic. And you are thinking, seriously, you should be me for a day. That would teach you a lesson. We must be aware that other people have emotions and they don't necessarily have to be the same as ours. We also have to have relationship management. That just means we must not react to others and deal with other people's energy. We have to learn to allow other people time and space to process their own emotions.

I want to focus on the power of managing our emotional intelligence in the first two components. Its two key things. First, it's an awareness of your feelings. I can't stress this enough. Remember, it's not about emotional elimination. It's about emotional control. Second, having the process to manage them.

For example. I could have the world's worst morning. Imagine I got up late, stubbed my toe on the way to the bathroom, got a flat tire on my way to my keynote, got in a fight with my husband on the phone, the worst morning ever. It doesn't really matter. Even after that, if I stood on stage and looked at my audience and told them I had a bad morning and wasn't feeling it so I am not doing my keynote... could you imagine! It doesn't matter what kind of morning I had. I still have to stand up there and do my shtick. And you know what? So do you. (And for the record, I would never have a fight with my husband. He is amazing!)

It's okay to have emotions, but we have to have an appropriate way to process them. Now, true confessions. This is where I get a little bit personal. I kind of tell on myself. Emotional control is not something that comes naturally to everyone. Especially me. I promise, it's a learned skill. My story is a lot real and little embarrassing. But I hope it helps you put it in perspective.

My personality style leans to well, a little wild. I tend to be a 90 miles an hour kind of person, all the time. I'm very type A. I'm a total and complete workaholic. 90 miles an hour, work, work, and work. I love it. I'm just going all the time. And because I tend to be like that, I do not have a lot of patience. I really don't. I try. I mean, I have absolutely zero tolerance. I mean, zero tolerance, especially for stupid people. And y'all, there are stupid people everywhere!

This is a real story of what not to do, but this is for me how this transition had to happen. I travel a lot for business. I spend a lot of time at airports. I spent a lot of time on airplanes. I just got to this place in my life, where the airport was my least favorite place on the planet. I was getting annoyed, irritated, and stressed out on my way to the airport in anticipation of how irritated, annoyed, and stressed out I was going to be once I arrived. I was proactively stressing. It was ridiculous because I would get to the airport and I'm like 90 miles an hour, right? It's like, all right, let's go. I got to get to the gate. I've got three phone calls, and 82 email I need to send before I get on the plane. So, let's go, let's go, and let's go! And I would get to the airport, and it felt like everyone and everything in it, was moving in slow motion!

The minute I arrive at the airport it is slow motion. And then I go to TSA and this is never a good thing. I have issues with TSA. No, no. Let me restate. TSA has issues with me. Y'all know what I mean, you go through, they check your ID, you go through and sometimes they let you pick a lane. I always try to pick the lane that looks like the most expedient, doesn't everyone? You're looking like, okay, lane one, family of eight, four strollers, no. Second lane, an old couple. They look like they have a combined age of 912, no. And it really doesn't matter which lane that I pick. I'm always in the slowest lane and apparently I make faces. So, I'm standing in the line with my face twisted up screaming silently, come on, let's go. Looking at the people in front of me thinking, laptop out of the bag dude! That dinner plate belt buckle is not going through, and that 64 ounce shampoo bottle is a big no! Come on people, speed it up!

I'm just getting more and more irritated. Now my mom says that this is why. I do not know if she is right, but it is true. I get randomly selected for additional screening all the time! So generally, if you see me at the airport, I'm probably at TSA, spread eagle getting patted down. And my whole theory is if I look irritated and annoyed, I'm sending a symbol, a subtle message to the TSA agent. Maybe we should speed this up? Clearly, I'm in a hurry. That is not how the TSA agents hear it. Apparently, that is not what they read. They think that means slow down and torture me. So, I'm already annoyed and I am barely through TSA. Now I'm speed walking to my gate and I am forever walking behind like the family of five.

Bless their hearts. They're all holding hands, taking up the entire walkway and walking at the pace of their toddler. I always feel like I'm a running back on a football team trying to find a hole in the line. I'm like, "Come on, come on. Let me get through. Let me get through." And I'm thinking, what are you people on vacation? They're all wearing Mickey Mouse ears, so maybe. I'm annoyed before I even get to the gate. And remember, this is not a good thing. This is the "what not to do." As I continue my run to the gate I come to the best thing and the worst thing at the airport, moving walkways. When you're a fast walker, those things rock. I'm like the bionic woman on those things. I love them. But I am forever behind the person that is lounging across the whole thing.

You know exactly what I'm talking about. There's a sign! Walk left. Stand right. Walk left. Stand right. I don't care if you stand. Just stand to the right. I'm walking through saying, "Come on people. This is not a ride. People let's go. I had one of the worst travel days. I was irritated and annoyed. I finally got to my hotel. When you need to that emotion out who do you call? When it's travel drama, I typically call my friend Rebecca because she's a speaker like I am. She totally appreciates the travel drama. So, I called her and I was so mad and I'm going off on my tangent on the phone saying, "I can't believe and this happened and that happened to me." Then she laughed at me.

I said, are you laughing at me? And she said," Yeah, you're funny." I said, "This is in no way funny." And in that moment, she said the words that we all hate to hear. She said, "You need to practice what you preach!" Then my former friend, Rebecca, no, I'm kidding. She's still my friend and I love her, but she was right. She reminded me that I need to think about my Steven Covey circles. Meaning, Steven Covey of *Seven Habits of Highly Effective People* fame. This is how he explains it.

We all have a small circle around us that is our circle of influence. These are the things in your life you have the power to influence, to change, to do something about. We all also have a bigger circle around us that is our circle of concern. Those are the things you can be concerned about but not necessarily change. When we are in those situations, when our emotions threaten to overwhelm us, emotional intelligence is needed. When the event happens, the trigger happens, the brain says bad, very, very bad, put up our impulse gate, reign in your horse. Pause. We're not going to react. We're going to respond. We're going to ask ourselves the question, is this my circle of influence or is this my circle of concern? You're taking back control. Now, think about it.

If you're in an emotional situation, something happens, and you decide it is your circle of influence, the question you ask yourself next is, what do you do? First step, you pause.

If this is my circle of influence, meaning you have the ability to influence what you do, you have to do something. If you have the ability to do something, do something. Don't be the person that complains and complains and complains and never does anything. We don't like those people. They're annoying.

I'll tell you where I think we struggle with this, is I think it's cultural. I think it's in our society. I think we are all or nothing people, we're go big or go home people. It's big, it's bold, it's broad. Everything is giant leaps and bounds. And I think because we tend to be all or nothing people, sometimes I think we see things in an all or nothing frame of mind.

I had a woman in my audience once, I had probably a hundred people in the room. She raised her hand and in front of everyone, said, "I hate my job. I am miserable." She said, "I dread going to work every day." She said, "It's giving me ulcers." She said, "I work with evil people. " She said, "My boss is the spawn of Satan." That was my favorite part. When she said that everybody laughed. And I looked at her and I said, "Woo that sounds bad. You better quit." When I told her that, what do you think she said to me? "Well, I can't." I said, "But why not? It sounds terrible!" She responded, "I have kids. I have bills. I have to put food on their table, a roof over their head and shoes on their feet!" I said, "Amen, sister. I appreciate that!"

See, think about what happened to her. She had, for whatever reason in her life, decided she only had two options in her life. Either option A, she had to stay and work at this horrible, awful job for the rest of her pathetic, miserable existence or option B, she quit tomorrow, was homeless living on the street and her children had no shoes. I'm like, "Holy cow, I would like option C please! There has to be something in the middle." We get so caught up in all or nothing thinking. When in reality, we have to look for small steps. What can you do?

If you want something to be different in your life, you have to do something different. And it doesn't have to be all or nothing. It doesn't have to be big giant leaps and bounds. Its small steps. We have to move from why we can't to how we can. What can we do? Small steps and take action. That is circle of concern.

What if the issue happens and you look at it and it feels like a circle of concern, and you think there is nothing you can do about it? What do you do then?

Let it go. You knew I was going there, right? Everybody sing it in true frozen fashion, let it go, let it go! It's so easy to say. So hard to do. I think that part of the challenge with this is that it's actually very similar. Remember I said we're all or nothing people. Well, the same thing happens here, we are all or nothing people.

Some people, when they are mad about something, are mad about it forever. They never let it go. They hold on to it forever. I had a woman one time, I was teaching a customer service session, and I had a woman tell me this very detailed, bad customer service story she had. She told the story and ended it by saying, "And I haven't stepped foot in a Sears store since." And that was 17 years ago.

I said, "Dang, that's a grudge right there." They probably have had a little employee turnover in 17 years. Maybe that is why they went out of business!

She told that story like it happened yesterday. Y'all there are a lot of people that will hold on to it forever.

Now we also have the flip side of that. Those people, the people who act like nothing ever bothers them. I call them, "It's okay. I'm okay, people. "Because they're the ones that always act like they are fine no matter what the issue is. We say, "Aren't you mad? I'd be mad." They respond with, "No, it's okay. I'm okay. No reason to be mad. Can't do anything about it. I'm a tree. I can bend. It's okay. I'm okay." Are they really okay? No, I don't think they're okay. They're what I call volcano people. They get mad and don't say anything for so long, eventually they blow. One random day you go ask them for a pencil and they lose their mind. It's never about the pencil. It's about everything else they've been mad about, but they haven't said anything and bottled up. Yes, things are going to frustrate us. We have to be okay with that.

I am going to lovingly call you out here. Because this is important. Remember, our goal is to make an impact on our lives and in the lives of the people we care about. When we can't control our emotions, we can't control anything. Your emotions are your choice, choose better.

Here is how I want you to think of this going forward. Here are some key takeaways that can help you to take back control of your emotions going forward. I adore my mom and she taught me some really valuable lessons that I don't think she had any idea were related to emotional intelligence.

There are three key things that my mom taught me that will change your life. First, my mom was very adamant about this for as long as I can remember, there's no such thing as a wrong emotion. And understand my mom came from a time before we had all of us getting in touch with our emotions, before we talked about emotional intelligence. Before there was Dr. Phil or Dr. Drew or Dr. Oz. Emotions were not talked about the same way, but she has always stood by the idea that there is no such thing as a wrong emotion. You can't tell someone their emotion is wrong and nobody can tell you that your emotion is wrong either.

To this day, if I say to my Mom, "Oh Mom, don't be mad about that. Don't let it get to you." She will respond with, "Don't tell me I can't be mad. It's my emotion. I can feel the way I want to feel." There's actually a lot of value in understanding this. Emotions are not math, meaning my emotion may be different than yours. We must be able to feel our feelings. You have to own your emotion. This is really critical because you cannot move past an emotion, get over a situation, or emotion until you have allowed yourself to feel it, to own it, to get all up in it. You have to feel it.

Sometimes that inner voice talks to us and tells us we should not be mad, we are wrong for feeling that way. Even telling ourselves that we are just stupid for being mad. The more you tell yourself you're stupid for feeling that way, it will take exponentially longer for you to move past it. The first step to emotional intelligence is there's no such thing as a wrong emotion. Stop telling yourself you're wrong for feeling that way. Own your emotion.

The second skill my Mom taught me, and she was very clear about this, we have to be able to vent it out. We have to do it at the appropriate place and appropriate time. We don't just explode randomly. Remember, I said we must process our emotions?

The process is: the event happens, that poke that makes our brain say bad very bad. We close our impulse gate and handle the situation appropriately and professionally. Then we go to our venting place of choice and open our impulse gate and let those emotions out. We vent them out. We feel them fully. And we don't beat ourselves up for feeling the way we feel. Instead of saying I am stupid for feeling this way, we say "I don't like that I am mad about this but I am going to get over it." That is emotional intelligence.

The third thing my Mom taught me that is absolutely amazing is you have to give yourself a time limit. You can be mad and feel your emotion but not forever. At some point you must let it go.

My mom has been doing this since I was a child. I did not get it until I became an adult, but she gives herself a time limit for how long she's allowed to be mad about something. Time limits can be different. Little things, shorter time limits, bigger things, and bigger time limits. My Mom has always done this. To this day, when my Mom gets really mad about something she calls me, and it's usually about my sister. But don't feel sorry for my sister, because she calls my sister when she's mad at me! And my sister and I call each other when we're mad at her. That's how we love. That's family love!

My mom will call me, "I'm so mad she said or she did." But then she will say, "But I have to be over it by three o'clock because that's my time limit." How does that work? But it does. And it's not because at three o'clock, she forgets it happened. It's because she chooses to move forward. She allows herself to own it and feel it and doesn't judge herself for what it is. She gives herself an opportunity to vent it, to say it, to feel it, to own it, and then she chooses to move forward. It's brilliant!

I do this at the airport now. This is my new method, my impulse gate is up to get me through TSA. Once I get through TSA, I get to open up my gate and I can be annoyed.

I can stomp around if I want to. I can huff and puff a little. I can call my sister and complain about the airport. But my time limit is the minute that I step onto that jet bridge and I get on that plane, I have to leave my mad at the airport. I have left mad at airports all across the country. It will be there for you when you get there. Trust me. But if I get on the plane and I start thinking about it again, I tell myself, no, I've already been mad about this. It's time to change my focus and think about something else and I choose to move forward. Now this is processing emotions effectively. It's okay to have them. It's okay to feel it. It's okay to vent it. It's not okay to have it forever.

I read a parable years ago that has always stuck with me and it is a great example of what I am saying to you. I simply love this story. It's a great way to really internalize what we're talking about here and why it's so important that we move through things.

This story is about two monks of the silent order. The silent order, meaning they cannot speak from sun up until sundown. So, the two monks of the silent order are walking through the forest and they come upon a creek. Standing on the bank of the creek is a woman and she's visibly agitated and frustrated. She's got this big dress with all these petticoats, a big hat, and a big basket of fruits and vegetables, and she's kind of mumbling to herself and she's mad. As soon as she sees the monks, she says, "Oh, good. You can help me. I need to get across the creek, but I don't want to get my dress wet." Well, of course the monks can't speak, but through hand gestures, they figure it out. One of the monks picks up her big basket of fruits and vegetables, and the other one picks up the woman, kind of flings her big dress and petticoats over his shoulder, and they slowly wade across the creek and gently set her down on the opposite bank. As soon as the monk puts the woman down, she shakes out her dress, adjusts her hat, grabs her basket, and takes off in a huff. No thank you. No, I appreciate your help. No you saved the day. Nothing. She just takes off in a huff. Of course, the monks can't speak, so they kind of shrug their shoulders and keep walking.

As soon as the sun sets, the monk that carried the basket looks at the monk who carried the woman and says, "Finally, I have been dying to talk to you! Can you believe that woman? After all we did to get her and that ridiculous dress and basket across the creek, and no thank you. No, I appreciate your help. No, you saved the day. You're my hero. Nothing. Can you believe that woman?" And the monk that carried the woman looked at the monk who carried the basket and said," Yeah, that was pretty bad, but you had it way worse than I did." The monk that carried the basket, looked at the monk who carried the woman and said," I don't know what you're talking about. I just had to carry the basket. You had to carry that woman in that ridiculous dress and hat?" The monk that carried the woman said, "Yes, that's true, but I only had to carry her across the creek. You've been carrying her all day."

Who are you carrying? And who do you need to drop in the creek? Y'all at some point, we have to let it go. There's that great saying, it's Gandhi, maybe it's Buddha, it might be Oprah, I can't remember, but it says," It's like drinking poison and expecting the other person to die." At some point, we have to choose to move forward. Your emotions are your emotions and only you can process them. No one can do it for you.

I talk about this a lot, and people often like to tell me that they get this, they are good at the emotions over the long haul. Because that is what this is, it is long term emotional intelligence. It isn't one and done. People like to say that their issue is in the heat of the moment, that's where they struggle.

Here's what I tell them. If you struggle losing your cool in the heat of the moment, it's directly linked to your over the long haul. They go together. This is how I explain it. Every single one of us on the inside, have what I call your emotional bucket. It's an emotional bucket and it sits on the inside by our heart. It's a holding area for all things emotion.

There are three layers in your emotional bucket. The bottom layer is what I call past traumas. We all have them. They can be anything. Maybe you went through a really horrible divorce. Maybe you had a really difficult childhood. Maybe you lost someone you loved, whatever it is, those are your past traumas. If you were to go to a therapist for it, they would probably tell you something along the lines of, you have to move through it. You can't hold onto it. Now, this doesn't mean you forget it. We're always going to carry it with us. It's always going to be a part of who we are. But we move through it, so it doesn't overflow our bucket. Because we have to have room for our other layers.

Your second layer is what I call your big current stressors. What are your big life stressors? That could be some financial challenges, maybe you've got a child who's struggling in school, health issues, whatever it is. The big life challenges. But here's the deal. Again, you can't let every stupid little thing stress you out, right? Because it would overflow your bucket. You can't be that person. Traffic is terrible. The line at the Starbucks is too long. No. Big stressors only because you still have to have room in your bucket for the top layer.

The top layer is what I call, whatever you're feeling right now. For example, right now, I'm mad at Joe until two o'clock. I'm mad at Matthew until four o'clock and I'm really mad at Terry until tomorrow at nine o'clock. (Remember our time limits?)

Here's the deal. I need to be over being mad at Joe at 2:00, don't I? Because I'm pretty sure Casey's going to do something that's going to make me mad and I'm going to need room in my bucket for her!

Emotional intelligence is the processing of emotions. It boils down to good bucket management. You gotta manage the bucket! That's how it works. Emotions come into your bucket and emotions go out of your bucket. Good bucket management is the key.

So, let's review the process.

The trigger happens.

Your brain says bad, very, very, bad.

Impulse gate, impulse gate, impulse gate.

Reign in your horse.

Handle the situation appropriately and professionally.

Go to your venting place of choice. Open up your impulse gate, vent it out, feel it, own it, all of those good things.

Then give yourself the time limit and chose to move on. Dump that bucket!

You have to allow that to happen. You really must empty your bucket. Because if you don't empty your bucket, think about what happens. In the heat of the moment, when that person is making you mad, you know you are feeling it, that anger or frustration, where does that anger go in the heat of the moment?

It sits in the top of your bucket. If your bucket is already overflowing with all the other stuff you have not let go of, where does the mad go? It explodes out. Volcano person.

You have heard the expression; people have a short fuse. What that means is they have a really full bucket.

We have to learn the emotional process, that good bucket management. Remember, emotions are not math. It's different for everyone. We have to acknowledge our emotions. We have to allow ourselves to feel them. They are intangible, but it's all about you having a process that allows you to manage them more effectively.

I promise, if you will learn to be empathetic with yourself and with others, it will change your emotional intelligence forever. I guarantee it.

Chapter 7

Grit, Grace, & Getting Back Up

(Because resilience is built, not born)

There's a strange and almost universal truth that most of us learn only after experience has knocked us around a few times. I know it took me a while to understand this basic truth. The moment you commit to something worthwhile, things get harder, not easier.

Think about it.

You decide to run a marathon. The first jog around the block feels empowering. But two weeks in, your knees ache, your lungs burn, and the voice in your head whispers, "You're not a runner. Why are you doing this?" Not that I would ever want to run a marathon! But as I have embraced a healthier lifestyle and have made moving my body part of my daily routine, I can testify to the truth of this feeling.

Maybe you start a new job and the first week feels like possibility and potential. Then week two arrives, and the workload doubles, the learning curve feels steep, and suddenly you're questioning whether you were even ready for this. I have a great friend that experienced this recently. She was excited about the possibility and the new challenges and all the amazing people she was getting to work with, and then the overwhelm set in. She is a tough cookie and of course battled through, but it is a very common feeling.

Or you launch a business or pursue a creative dream, and in the beginning it feels electric. But soon the deadlines, bills, and self-doubt show up, and you realize the road is full of potholes you couldn't have seen from the starting line.

It's almost as if the universe has a sense of humor: the second you declare, "I want to grow, I want to change, I want to achieve something bigger," it responds with, "Great, let's see how badly you want it." And the challenge is on. Back to the Dojo.

One of the greatest lessons I have learned is that hard is not a sign you're on the wrong path. Hard is the path.

This is where resilience and grit come in. If we want to see our goals through to fruition, if we want to become the kind of people who don't just start but actually finish, we have to cultivate the ability to withstand difficulty, push through frustration, and keep moving forward even when everything in us wants to quit.

And that's where most people fall off track—not because they aren't smart enough, talented enough, or capable enough. But because they never learned the most important skill of all: how to keep going when it gets hard. That is true grit.

At its core, resilience is basically frustration tolerance. It's the ability to sit with discomfort, to stay in the messy middle, and to resist the temptation to quit when progress doesn't come quickly enough. It is the time in the training ground, remember the Dojo?

Frustration tolerance doesn't sound glamorous, but it is required for success. And if you think about it, nearly every success story is really a story of frustration tolerance:

Thomas Edison tried thousands of times to make the lightbulb work. Most of those attempts ended in failure. What separated him from the countless inventors who quit was his tolerance for frustration. Each failed filament wasn't the end, it was simply more information.

J.K. Rowling was rejected by a dozen publishers before Harry Potter found its home. Imagine the frustration of being told no repeatedly when you believe deeply in your story. Most people would have stopped after the first or second rejection. She tolerated the frustration and the world is richer for it. And so is she!

I was watching a documentary about how big cats hunt for food. They spend hours stalking and hunting their prey and nine out of ten hunts fail. The key is they only need one! And that is true for us as well. We will spend a lot of time in frustration and making slow progress, but we only need one step forward at a time.

Resilience is not about pretending difficulties don't exist. It's about developing the muscle to endure them without giving up. Think about this, what does resilience feel like? We all want to be more resilient, it is very hot topic these days, but what does it actually feel like? Here is the headline, resilience doesn't feel good! It feels frustrating.

When we think about frustration tolerance, I think it is helpful to think of it as having a threshold. Some people have a very low threshold: the moment they encounter resistance, they back away. Others have a high threshold: they can withstand discomfort for long stretches, trusting that eventually something will give. The good news? Your threshold is not set in stone. Frustration tolerance is something we can learn to expand.

Have you ever heard the expression, "I'm a tree I can bend?" I love that saying! What it means is when storms hit, some trees snap while others bend. The difference isn't the strength of the storm, it's the flexibility of the tree. Resilient people aren't made of steel; they bend, they sway, they adapt, but they don't break.

Psychologists studying resilience have noticed key patterns in those who recover from setbacks and keep going. When we understand and work on these four things we can build our frustration tolerance.

First, expect difficulty. Resilient people don't go into challenges assuming it will be smooth sailing. They anticipate obstacles, which means they're less shocked when hardship arrives. They don't say, "Why is this happening to me?" but instead we teach ourselves to say, "Of course it's hard—this is the process." I am always reminded of the movie "A League of

Their Own" where Tom Hanks says to Geena Davis "If it were easy, everyone would do it!"

Second, separate failure from identity. When a resilient person fails at something, they don't see it as proof that they are a failure. They see it as data. This mindset shift makes frustration less personal and more tolerable. Everyone fails sometimes, successful people don't dwell on it they learn from it.

Third, have perspective. In the middle of a challenge, it's easy to feel like this setback is the end of the world. Resilient people zoom out. They know today's obstacle will look small in the rearview mirror, and that helps them endure it now.

Lastly, learn to connect struggle to growth. Resilient people believe hardship is shaping them, not destroying them. They see difficulty as the weight that builds their strength.

When you understand that resilience is really about flexibility and frustration tolerance, you can start to reframe the hard parts of life as opportunities—not punishment. It is about pushing through the training ground and not giving up when it gets hard.

The Role of Setbacks in Growth

There's a universal pattern in human achievement that shows we often overlook how setbacks don't have to be an interruption to the journey but instead, setbacks are the journey.

Think of anyone you admire for their strength, character, or accomplishments. Their story is not a straight line upward. It's a jagged path full of detours, dead ends, and restarts. And yet, when we face our own setbacks, we often believe we've done something wrong, that the detour is proof we aren't cut out for it so we give up on our big goal or plan.

But what if we saw setbacks for what they really are — a training ground for resilience?

Every time you face frustration and choose not to quit, you are literally building your capacity for grit. Every time you stumble, get back up, and keep moving forward, you are wiring your brain to believe that you can handle hard things.

Those of you that know me may know that I am a huge Sylvester Stallone fan. I mean HUGE. I have loved him as long as I can remember. And one of his greatest monologues was as Rocky Balboa, he told his son, "Let me tell you something you already know. The world ain't all sunshine and rainbows. It's a very mean and nasty place and I don't care how tough you are, it will beat you to your knees and keep you there permanently if you let it. You, me, or nobody is gonna hit as hard as life. But it ain't about how hard ya hit. It's about how hard you can get hit and keep moving forward. How much you can take and keep moving forward. That's how winning is done! Now if you know what you're worth then go out and get what you're worth. But ya gotta be willing to take the hits and not pointing fingers saying you ain't where you wanna be because of him, or her, or anybody! Cowards do that and that ain't you! You're better than that! I'm always gonna love you no matter what. No matter what happens. You're my son and you're my blood. You're the best thing in my life. But until you start believing in yourself, ya ain't gonna have a life."

Poor grammar aside, he is spot on! Setbacks provide practice reps for frustration tolerance. They force us to develop patience, creativity, and problem-solving. And when we finally reach our goal, we're not just proud of the outcome, we're proud of the person we became along the way.

It's worth asking: if things inevitably get hard, why bother starting at all? Why put ourselves through the struggle? I believe the gift is hidden in the hard. The very struggle we wish we could avoid is the thing that transforms us. The challenge is the Dojo, the training ground and the difficulty is the trainer. The hardship is the fire that forges resilience and grit.

This doesn't mean we enjoy every moment. Nobody loves frustration, setbacks, or failures in the moment. But over time, we come to realize that the very moments we wanted to escape were the moments that helped us to grow the most. During some of the most difficult times in my life I wanted to quit, but once I came out on the other side, I was proud of who I became in the process.

Resilience isn't just about surviving life's difficulties. It's about being shaped by them into someone stronger, braver, and more capable than you were before.

The Power of Attitudes and Actions

I often pose the question to my audience "What do you control?" Of course, the answer is basically your attitudes and your actions. We control our responses, our reactions, our thoughts, our behaviors, but basically it boils down to our attitudes and actions.

Let's start with our attitude. If resilience is the engine that keeps us moving through hard things, then our attitudes are the steering wheel. They determine where we focus, how we interpret challenges, and whether we respond with despair or with determination.

The truth is, most of us underestimate the role of attitude. We think success is about raw talent, the right opportunities, or maybe just sheer luck. But study after study—and countless lived experiences—tell us that it's our attitude toward struggle that makes the difference between someone who gives up and someone who breaks through.

Think of it this way: two people can go through the exact same circumstance, say, losing a job, failing an exam, or hitting a setback in business, and walk away with completely different outcomes. One person spirals into defeat, seeing the event as proof they are worthless. The other reframes the setback as a challenge to learn from and emerges stronger. The difference isn't the event—it's the attitude they brought to it.

I use this example. I travel a lot for business, so I fly quite a bit. So, let's say I am flying home to Dallas and my husband is going to pick me up at the airport. Just go with me on this, because it isn't going to happen. But we'll pretend! So, there I am, I get off the plane and he is standing there with a big bouquet of flowers! And I think, "Aww, he loves me!" Now, the same event can happen, I get off the plane there he is with that big bouquet of flowers, and I think, "Hey! What did he do wrong?" Same event but based on my own frame of reference and life experiences the reaction can be very different.

So, if we want to build resilience and grit, we must become intentional about the attitudes we cultivate.

I think there are two key areas we can focus on to be better: forgiveness and happiness.

Forgiveness: Releasing the Weight of the Past

Resilience isn't just about how we handle the present moment, it's also about what we carry with us from the past. And few things weigh us down more than bitterness, resentment, or regret.

When we hold onto anger, whether toward ourselves or others, we drain energy we could use for forward motion. Imagine trying to run a race while dragging a heavy backpack full of rocks. That's what unforgiveness does. It slows us down, exhausts us, and makes even small challenges feel unbearable.

Forgiveness, then, is not about excusing bad behavior or pretending something didn't hurt. It's about setting ourselves free from the weight of the past so we can move forward unencumbered.

Psychologists have found that forgiveness is linked to lower stress, better physical health, and greater life satisfaction. But beyond the science, there's a practical truth: you cannot grit your way through the future if you're chained to the past.

Forgiveness of others allows us to stop replaying old hurts and redirect that energy into building resilience for what's ahead.

Forgiveness of ourselves allows us to accept that mistakes are part of the process. Instead of being paralyzed by guilt or shame, we can use failure as fuel for growth.

Think about the people you admire most for their resilience. Chances are, they've faced deep hurt or disappointment, but they didn't let bitterness consume them. They forgave, released, and kept moving. That's what made their grit possible.

Happiness: Fuel for Endurance

At first glance, happiness and grit don't seem to belong in the same sentence. We often imagine grit as grinding, suffering, and teeth-gritted determination. But here's the paradox: happiness is one of the most powerful sources of resilience we have.

Why? Because when we cultivate happiness, joy, gratitude, optimism, we build an emotional reservoir that sustains us when things get hard.

Think of happiness as fuel. When you're running on empty, every obstacle feels insurmountable. But when your tank is full, you have the reserves to push through difficulty.

I have no doubt that people who regularly practice gratitude, savor joy, and nurture positive emotions are more resilient. They bounce back faster, not because life is easier for them, but because they have built up emotional strength.

Happiness doesn't mean denying pain or pretending everything is fine. It means intentionally looking for the good, even in the midst of struggle. It means pausing to celebrate progress, however small. It means remembering that joy and hardship can coexist.

Resilient people aren't happy because life is easy. They're happy because they've chosen to see and savor what's good, even when life is hard. And that happiness gives them the grit to keep going.

How Attitudes Shape Outcomes

It's one thing to understand forgiveness and happiness in theory. It's another to see how they actually change our lives in practice.

For example, a person who forgives doesn't waste years on bitterness, instead they're free to build something new. Just like a person who cultivates happiness doesn't burn out as quickly because they have joy to fuel their grit. Know this, attitudes aren't fluffy extras. They are the foundation of resilience.

Choosing Your Attitude

The best news of all is attitudes are choices. We may not choose the circumstances we face, but we always choose the lens through which we see them. You choose your attitude. Every day, in small moments, we decide things like will I forgive or hold a grudge? Will I look for joy or dwell on misery?

Each choice strengthens or weakens our resilience. And over time, these daily choices accumulate into grit.

The world will always present us with challenges we cannot control. But our attitudes? Those belong to us. And when we choose wisely, we arm ourselves with the mindset needed to not only survive difficulty, but to thrive through it.

Chapter 8

Say the Thing

(Communication, courage, and using your voice)

If your impact is your superpower, then your voice is how you use it. And yet, this is where so many of us play small. We stay quiet when we should speak up. We soften our message so much it loses meaning. We wait until we feel "ready," "confident," or "perfect," which, let's be honest, rarely happens. Instead, we let the noise in our head take over: What if I say it wrong? What if they don't like it? What if I look stupid? "No one cares anyway." So, we shrink. We hesitate. We stay safe. And in doing that, we don't just hold back our words. We hold back our impact. Because the truth is, your ability to communicate clearly, honestly, and even when your voice shakes, is directly tied to your ability to lead your life on purpose.

When you learn to speak up anyway, to be real instead of rehearsed, and to say what needs to be said even when it feels uncomfortable, you step into ownership of your life. And that's where your impact starts to show up, not just for you, but for every person your voice was meant to reach.

I believe it is not enough to think about making an impact, you have to be willing to speak your impact.

But here's where most people get it wrong. Speaking up isn't just about saying something, it's about saying something that actually moves things forward. If your communication doesn't lead to clarity, resolution, or progress, then all you've done is create noise. High-impact communication is results-oriented. It's not about winning the argument, proving your point, or getting the last word. It's about asking yourself: What outcome do I actually want here? Because when you get clear on that, it changes how you show up in the conversation. You stop reacting, and you start communicating with purpose.

And let's talk about defensiveness for a second—because this is where we derail ourselves fast. Someone says something we don't like, and immediately we're in protection mode. We interrupt. We justify. We explain. We shut down or we fire back. And the second we do that, we stop listening, and when we stop listening, we stop learning, we stop connecting, and we stop solving the problem. If you want to communicate with impact, you have to be willing to lean in instead of armor up. Trust me, I speak from years of experience on this. I spent way too many years hurting a lot of feelings, hurting people I cared about because I couldn't figure out how to stop getting defensive and shut up and listen.

Curiosity is one of the most powerful tools you have. Help me understand. Tell me more. Walk me through that. Those kinds of responses don't make you weak—they make you effective. Because now you're actually getting to the root of the issue instead of just reacting to the surface. When I learned how to embrace this, it made a huge difference. In my relationships and with my stress.

Another place we lose our impact? We let things build. We don't say anything when something bothers us, we brush it off, we "let it go." Then we keep letting it go... and letting it go... until suddenly we are not calm, collected, or constructive—we are a walking emotional explosion waiting for the wrong moment. And then when it finally comes out, it doesn't come out as thoughtful communication—it comes out as frustration, sarcasm, or overwhelm. That's not communication. That's release. And while it might feel good for a minute, it rarely leads to the outcome you actually want.

High-impact communicators don't avoid issues, they address them. But they address them with intention. The goal is not to escalate a situation, it's to resolve the situation. That means being clear instead of passive, direct instead of dramatic, and focused instead of emotional. It means saying, "Hey, this matters, and I want to work through it," instead of pretending it doesn't exist until it becomes a bigger problem. Because every time you choose not to say something that needs to be said, you are choosing short-term comfort over long-term impact.

And here's the bottom line: if you want to make a real impact, in your career, your relationships, your leadership, your life, you cannot outsource your voice. You must be willing to speak up for yourself and not rely on others to do it for you. You cannot wait for the perfect moment, the perfect wording, or the perfect confidence level. You have to be willing to speak up, lean in, stay curious, and communicate with intention. Because your impact doesn't just come from what you know or what you do, it comes from what you're willing to say, how you say it, and whether you say it at all.

Let me lovingly call you out for a minute... because if you're reading this thinking, "Yeah, but that's just not me. I'm not confrontational. I don't like conflict. I'd rather just keep the peace," What I hear is that you've gotten really good at avoiding discomfort and not communicating with impact. And I get it. It feels easier in the moment. But let's be honest, how's that working for you? Because every time you stay quiet when something needs to be said, every time you water down your message so no one gets uncomfortable, every time you choose silence over clarity, you're not keeping the peace... you're just postponing the problem. And usually, you're the one paying for it, through frustration, resentment, missed opportunities, and conversations that never happen but absolutely should. Avoiding the conversation doesn't protect your impact — instead it limits it. And at some point, if you really want to make a difference in your life and in the lives of others, you have to decide that a little discomfort in the moment is worth a whole lot more than staying stuck in patterns that aren't serving you. I don't just want you to hypothetically understand the importance of communication, I want to arm you with real tools that will help make an impact. That is my goal for this chapter. So, let's get to it!

Results-Oriented Communication

People say, "Why do I have to be more tactful? Why do I have to be professional? Why do I have to be diplomatic?" And it is because it's all about results. I always tell people, "I don't talk just to hear myself talk." Although my husband would argue that point. I think it's about results. I think if we're going to take the time, the risk, the energy of having a conversation with someone, then we want something on the other end.

The idea is we want to communicate with tact, professionalism, and diplomacy. But what the hell does that even mean? I have no doubt if I asked people, "Do you know what tact, professionalism, and diplomacy means?" everyone would say yes. But if I actually required you to define it using actual words, we struggle. And if you think I am making this up, know that I have tried these in countless training sessions. It is a fact. Once people start to think about it and how they would define it, it comes, but it is not nearly as easy as people initially think it will be.

Go ahead and try it. I will wait. Stop reading for a minute. And think about how you would define the word tact, the word professionalism, and the word diplomacy. It's OK. I will wait.

What did you come up with? My hope is that by having the opportunity to say it out loud, even to yourself, you had to really put it into words. It helped clarify it for you. Maybe even gave you pause. I mean, you know it when you see it, right? We have all said at least once, "Well, that wasn't very tactful!"

I want to make sure we're on the same page, so what is tact? There's lots of things you might have thought of. You might have thought it's being sensitive. It's sugarcoating it. It's making the pill go down easier. That's what I always think of anyway. It's saying things in a nice way. It's giving bad news and still doing it politely. It's being non-offensive. Those are all things we think of with tact. And those are all right. I think all of those are good things to think about and consider.

For me, tact boils down to this. It's not just what you say. It's how you say it. Isn't that the essence of tact? It's not just what you say. It's how you say it. You can tell people no. You can tell people they're not going to get what they want. You're going to tell them that that's not the way it's going to be. But it's not just what you say. It's how you say it. That's the difference. And isn't it true that you can say the right words and say them the wrong way? It's all about how you communicate the information. It's being honest. It's being truthful, but it's being tactful. And I will tell you, and I know I'm not the only one in the world who have known people that like to say, "I'm just honest. I just tell it like it is. If they didn't want to know, why did they ask me?" Let me tell you what I say to those people.

Honesty is beautiful. But honesty does not make you a good communicator. In the real world, you have to learn to balance honesty with a little thing we call tact. You have to combine those. It's not just what you say. It's how you say it. That is tact.

Professionalism

Let's talk professionalism. Think about some of the things you thought about for professionalism. I personally think this is the hardest one to define because it can mean different things to different people. When I ask what people think professionalism means, I tend to hear it's how you present yourself. It's how you carry yourself. It's your experience or your knowledge. It's how you dress. It's how you show up in a room.

All those things combined make professional. Here's what I think is interesting about professionalism because it is the whole package. It's how you present yourself. It's the whole package, isn't it? But it's different in different situations for different people.

I always think about a hospital. Let's say you go to a hospital, and you get on an elevator. A guy gets on the elevator behind you and let's say he's wearing some scrubs and some tennis shoes, maybe a white coat. Maybe he's got a stethoscope around his neck. You would probably look at him and say, "Oooh, very professional." Very professional. He probably knows where the cafeteria is, right? Very professional. But if I was doing a big keynote for a room full of a thousand bankers, and I walked on stage wearing scrubs and some tennis shoes. I would be very comfortable, but not very professional. (I wouldn't mind changing that rule up just a little bit!)

Professionalism is big picture. It's how we communicate in all the different avenues of communication. It's how we present ourselves and it encompasses a lot of things.

It's a lot about perception. This is what I call a foundation principle in communication.

Communication is not just about what you say. It's about what is heard.

Haven't y'all had that conversation with someone when you walked away thinking they have no idea what I just said? You knew just that conversation was going to come back to you. You feel like you are speaking a foreign language. That's the problem. It's not just about good intentions. Of course, good intentions are important, but good intentions are not enough. If we are talking about results-oriented communication, we must take accountability for the effectiveness of our communication.

We have all met the person that constantly complains that they are being misunderstood. Everyone else gets it wrong. It is not their fault, it is everyone else. At some point we have to realize, what is the common denominator there? Maybe it's not everyone else, maybe it's them? It's time to do the check up from the neck up!

I think of it as a big old giant slinky. A slinky is a really good visual for what communication is all about. When you pull the slinky out, it's a big old giant spiral, right? That is what communication looks like. Every time you enter into a conversation with someone, you come in in the middle of the spiral. And it's from the minute that that conversation begins, we either start to have positive upward spiral communication or negative downward spiral communication. My guess is you have experienced both. What makes the difference between positive, upward and negative downward? Lots of things contribute to that, of course, but there's a couple that I think are extremely important.

First, it's that feeling of rapport. Just that feeling you get about people. For example, when you meet someone for the first time, and it could be anywhere. You could be at a party, you could be at church, sitting in my audience at a conference-- and you're sitting next to someone you've never met before, and I made you talk to them and share with them against your will. So, you know when you meet someone for the first time, you don't know why. You can't explain it. You just get that feeling about them and you just don't like them? Or you do like them. It works both ways. But that feeling you get about people, that's rapport.

When positive rapport is there, we tend to have more positive communication. My guess is, everyone has people that you work with that you have natural rapport with. You can just talk to them. It's just easy to have a conversation. Even if it's not great news, you can talk to them, and it works out OK. It's all good. And then there's other people. It feels like no matter what the conversation is about, you can say to them, "I love that jacket." And they say, "What? What's wrong with it? What?" No matter what, it is negative. When the rapport's not there, your job is to build it. If it's not there naturally, you have to craft it. You have to create it. If you build it, they will come. When you lean in with curiosity and look for common ground we can build that rapport.

The second thing that makes a difference between positive upward spiral communication and negative downward spiral is feedback. Have you noticed that we change how we communicate based on the feedback we receive from the other person? For example, you and I are standing there and we're having a conversation. And as you and I are talking, I'm standing there with my arms crossed in front of me, leaning back a little, arms crossed in front of me. Think about what we have heard that means. Closed off, distancing myself, not interested, defensive. Of course, that is not always true. It could mean you're cold or it could be a comfortable way to stand. Someone told me one time it's to cover up the fat rolls. I like that one. Think about that though. If you and I are having that conversation and I'm standing there with my arms crossed because I'm cold or having a fat day, you might sense negativity. You're probably not going to say anything. You may not even be able to pinpoint what the problem is, you're just going to sense negativity. When you sense negativity from someone, think about how you continue to talk to them. You are going to get snippy. You know what snippy is, It's a technical term. Google it. Snippy. It's like snarky, snotty, snobby. If in a conversation someone gets snippy with me, guess what I am going to have to do? Oh, you know, I am getting snippy back. Now we have snippy talking to snippy and that never works. It makes a difference if we pay attention, not just to the messages we're sending, but to the messages of the person that we're talking to.

As we can see, communication is much bigger than just the words we say. In any communication process, there are three pieces. I am sure a lot of you have heard this before, it's pretty much communication 101. But it is important and is exactly what we are talking about here. In any communication process, there are three parts. The sender, which is the person sending the message, the receiver, who is the person receiving it, and the message itself. The message itself is made up of three Vs. It's easy to remember. There's the visual part of the message. That's your facial expressions and your body language. The vocal is your emotional intonation. It's your tone of voice. And if any of you have teenagers, you know they've mastered the tone of voice. They're learning it young! Tone of voice is critical. And then of course, the verbal are the words that we actually say. I always think about it like this. Those three Vs have to be congruent. They have to be sending the same message because if the message is mixed, it's a gamble. Which one are people going to believe? And you can change the meaning of the words by changing the tone.

That's the problem. We're looking for a congruent message. Our words have to match our tone and our tone has to match the visual message. When they don't they send a mixed message and can impact our professionalism, our credibility, and the respect we receive from others. Believe it or not all those things are communicated through all three of those V's. You can say the right words, but if you roll your eyes when you say them, it changes the meaning. You can say the right words, but if you change your tone, it doesn't matter. And I'm a big believer that tone gives us away more often than not. I do a lot of customer service work. And I will tell you that is to me, one of the single biggest mistakes that people make in customer service. If you work in a company and you have a customer service team, you watch the tone. You can give them a script. Oh, they can read a script. They'll read it for you. They'll read it word for word. But if that tone starts to shift all of a sudden it sounds different. We have to make sure all three of those V's are saying the same thing.

So tactful, it's not just what you say, it's how you say it. Professionalism is making sure we're sending a clear, concise, congruent message of professionalism through all three Vs.

Diplomacy

Let's look at the importance of diplomacy. Diplomacy is interesting. When I think of diplomacy I think about a diplomat. Countries have diplomats. What is a diplomat's job? No one knows. No, a diplomat's job is to represent their country and work with other diplomats in areas of mutual interest. That's what diplomacy is all about.

It's about things like balance. It's about our willingness to listen. Listening is the key to diplomacy. We must be willing to listen.

This does not mean that we have no feelings. It doesn't mean that we don't care about other people. I think it's the opposite. I think it is showing concern. I think of diplomacy as three basic components. I think you must be able to communicate your position. You must be able to communicate what the issue is. You must be able to communicate what the consequences of said incidents will be. You must be able to state your position.

Then you must be willing to listen to theirs. I know. Listen, really? Do you have to? Yeah, you really do. You really want to listen because once we listen, then we can negotiate to a solution. And that is the third part of diplomacy. Remember, 1. State your position, 2. Listen to theirs, and 3. Negotiate to solution.

Keep in mind, a very basic human need is to feel valued. We all want to feel valued. Humans want to believe that what we say or do, or feel, matters. So how do we communicate that message to others? And one of the best ways to do it is to genuinely listen to what they have to say, and then we can negotiate or navigate to a solution. Remember though, you still want to know your bottom line. You need to know your unique position. Your minimum acceptable outcome, your parameters, your bottom line.

Think of it like this. Let's say you're buying a car. So, before you walk on that car lot, aren't you going to have a number in your head? You're going to have a number, a dollar amount of how much you're willing to spend on that car. And you really need to have a number because imagine if you didn't?!

You'd walk onto the car lot on a mission, and the salesman would ask you, "So, how much are you looking to spend?" And all you would be able to say is, "Well, I don't know. Surprise me." You would probably get a pretty sweet ride, but you'd probably pay way too much! The importance of understanding your bottom line is critical. Then you have to communicate that to others tactfully and professionally, and you have to be willing to listen to theirs. Then we can negotiate.

We understand the importance of tactful, professional, and diplomatic communication on our ability to impact our life and the lives of others. We agree we should do that and we have an idea of what that means. But how does it actually sound? What are the basic communication techniques that can be used in those uncomfortable situations?

It wouldn't make sense to tell you that you need to speak up and make your voice heard if I didn't give you ideas on how to do that. So, I want to make sure that if you are reading this, that you get some very specific language that you can use to help make even the most difficult conversations more impactful.

We need a sample scenario we can play with to give us a way to implement a few specific techniques. I use this scenario in my workshops all the time, mostly because this is one situation that thousands of people have told me they have dealt with. It is also just a way to illustrate the techniques. The techniques can be used a million different ways once you know what they are.

Let's do it! I want you to pretend that you're in a meeting and you say something, share an idea, offer a suggestion or solution. Then a coworker across the table snaps at you in a rude, insulting, and sarcastic tone of voice. You're in a meeting so everyone else hears it. What would you do?

There are two questions I would consider. Do you say something right then or do you say something later and then what do you say? Keep in mind, there's more than one right answer. (There are some wrong answers too, but there are lots of right answers!)

Generally, your response can be determined by whether you lean a little bit more passive in your communication or you lean a little bit more aggressive in your communication.

If you picture communication falling on a spectrum. On one end of the spectrum you have passive, the other end is aggressive, and in the middle is assertive. Know this, no one is either passive or assertive or aggressive. We can be all of them. It can depend on the situation, your level of comfort with the person, how tired you are, and how many people have messed with you that day, a whole host of factors.

We can communicate and behave in all three. We learn as we go through life what works, what doesn't work, what is comfortable and what is not comfortable. Then we can move up and down the spectrum of passive, assertive, or aggressive depending on what you perceive the situation to call for.

Even though we are not exclusively passive, assertive or aggressive and we can communicate and behave in all of them, we do naturally lean one way or the other.

In difficult and dicey situations, those high stress situations, when the heat is on, we feel challenged or confronted, whichever way we lean tends to show up in stress. It is similar to the flight or fight mindset. Do we lean aggressive and fight? Or do we tend to lean passive and run?

Whichever way we lean is what kind of starts to come out. When people lean a bit more passive, they tend to be likely to shut down and not say anything. Their whole approach is they don't want to make it worse. So, they say nothing.

People that tend to lean a little to the aggressive side tend to believe they have to defend themselves. When they get challenged or confronted they snap back. They are ready for a fight.

Neither of these approaches are very effective. We want to find a balance, the meet in the middle. We want to speak up and be heard, let them know we heard them but we don't want to escalate the situation.

My all-time favorite technique. I promise you, if you learn one technique from me in this book, learn this one. I promise you it will change your life because when you get comfortable with this, you will be amazed at how well it works. The technique is called Acknowledge Transition. Basically, you acknowledge what the person said, and then you transition back to where you want to be.

In this specific situation it might sound like this: "That sounds like something we should probably talk about after the meeting. Let's stay on track for now. As I was saying..." and keep going.

Because I really want this to work for you, I want to make sure that we're clear on the details. When you acknowledge, you look at the person. When you transition, you look away from them. The other tip is this should be a big, long, giant run-on sentence. "...As I was saying..." and you keep talking, because if you don't, they will.

This is what I hear people worry about when they try this technique. That in the heat of the moment, people worry that if they said that, they would forget what they were saying. Here's what you can do. Instead of saying as "I" was saying, you can actually turn the floor over to someone else. You could say, "Frank, that sounds like something we should probably talk about after the meeting. Let's stay on track for now. Jim, what do you think about what we were talking about?" Yes. Throw Jim under the bus. Right off the curb. Let Jim read my book. You can also just say, where were we or what's the next item on the agenda. Basically, turning the floor back to the group.

When I say this is my favorite technique, holy smokes, I am not kidding. You can use this technique a thousand ways. In negotiation, in dicey conversations, in regular conversations, it works so well. It is the ultimate diplomatic communication technique.

Remember, we said we state our position then we listen to theirs. When they finish their thought, we can Acknowledge Transition. Acknowledge what they said, it could sound like: I understand where you are coming from, I hear you, that makes sense, I understand you feel that way, I understand you see it that way, I understand you disagree with me, I understand you think I am wrong, I understand you are mad, the list is endless!

Then we transition back toward resolution or solution. The transition could be, "here is what I think we can do from here..." or anything like that. It is a fantastic technique to move the conversation along.

I promise you, once you start using it. You will love it.

One of the biggest mistakes I think we see in today's culture and environment, not just in the workplace but in our lives is our approach to disagreements. We seem to have gotten to this strange place where we are not allowed to disagree with someone. Oh, there is a lot of disagreement out there, but it tends to be loud and obnoxious and polarizing. So, the conclusion has been made by many that any form of disagreement either means you can no longer talk to that person and you must hate them or you are just not allowed to speak your mind, you keep your mouth shut and never share a counter idea. This is bullshit. We must get better about being OK with people who disagree with us. Not everyone sees things the same way and that is a good thing. It becomes a bad thing when we can't appropriately discuss differences in a productive way. Making an impact means being open to sharing your thoughts, your opinions, and your ideas. Even when people disagree. Who knows, maybe you will make an impact and change their mind? This is only going to happen if we can disagree and communicate through it.

You can change up the Acknowledge Transition technique into an Acknowledge Question technique so easily and it is a great way to disagree diplomatically. The Acknowledge statement can be something like, I actually disagree with that, I see it differently, that's not the way I see it, or I have a different perspective, anything along those lines. Then we add the Question piece to complete it. The questions can be anything that allows you to lean in with curiosity and gather information rather than being argumentative. It could be, tell me more about that, help me to understand your position, or walk me through your thought process. When you combine them you have a powerful, tactful and diplomatic communication technique!

Along the lines of people's apparent fear of conflict and disagreement, comes a fear that to say something would escalate the emotion and turn it into a fight making it much worse. I understand the concern, however, if you aren't willing to speak up and do it in the name of keeping the peace you are really only keeping the tension. (Did you catch that great Acknowledge Transition sentence there?)

When people are aggressive in their communication they tend to make those big, bold, broad, generic nothing statements. But they say them loud and wag their finger, lean in and look like they are getting closer to you... let's face it. They scare us into submission. Those alarm bells go off and we tend to shut down. This is not the time to shut down, this is the time to lean in. With curiosity, of course!

The best communicators out there have gotten comfortable asking the question, "is that how you meant that?" So, you start it with the Acknowledge statement—something like, "Wow, Frank, that felt like a personal attack, is that how you meant it?" Or, "Wow, Frank, that felt really negative, is that how you meant it?" It's a beautiful way to get that difficult person a little off kilter. They will pause and probably lie to you!

And when I say they will lie to you that means they will respond with something like, "No, I'm not trying to be negative it's just this project/idea/issue is ridiculous!" Or "No, I am not attacking you I am just mad about this...!" That is wonderful. Now all we have to do is Acknowledge

Transition and get them back on topic. That could sound like, "Oh I am so glad I was wrong; we can talk about that project/budget/issue whatever it is."

Keep in mind there is the message the person is communicating with and there is the emotion with which they are communicating. When people are emotionally charged and they lash out, we tend to focus on that emotion. That becomes what we respond to. If instead you can lean in with curiosity and focus on the words and not the emotions, you can de-escalate the situation and redirect the conversation.

Now, I want to share one more technique with you. I love this technique, but it can be a little scary if you are not as comfortable being that impactful communicator. But stay with me, I promise if you try it you will love it!

This technique is called perception checking. Perception checking is basically three components. The idea is, as assertive communicators, as tactful, professional and diplomatic communicators, we would never assume what people mean by what they say. We always check our own perceptions.

Perception Checking is a three step process. Step one, state your observation. Gee, I've noticed in the last few minutes that we've been talking, you've looked at your watch eight times. Gee, I noticed when I said that, you rolled your eyes at me. State your observation. Step number two, share your interpretation of it. To me, that says that you're not interested in what I'm saying. To me, that says you disagree with what I'm saying. Step number three, confirm. Am I right?

Now think about how that works. I was checking into a hotel one day and as I was being checked in I was asking a lot of questions. I was doing the opening keynote at a conference in that hotel first thing in the morning so I was asking if the ballroom was set up, could I look at it, was the AV team there, things like that. Apparently, I asked her too many questions because she was rolling her eyes at me. She did it several times and I finally got annoyed with it, so I Perception Checked her. I said, "I noticed when I asked that you rolled your eyes at me. To me that says you thought that was a stupid question. Am I right?" She about choked. Her eyes grew to dinner plate size, and she said she didn't even realize she was rolling her eyes. Then she proceeded to politely answer all my questions without ever blinking. I think she was afraid to blink! It was so funny to watch!

Now, if they don't lie to you, they are going to tell you the truth. And I want you armed and ready for that too!

I was doing a customer service workshop for a city. I had about 150 city employees in the room from all different city departments. Parks and Rec, Utilities, Police, Fire, I even had the librarian. You would think the librarian would be nice, right? No. Not at all.

It was a full day workshop and before we even got to the first break the librarian kept rolling her eyes at me. It felt like no matter what I said she disagreed. She rolled her eyes one too many times! So, I Perception checked her in front of the entire room. I said, "Now I noticed when I said that you rolled your eyes at me. To me that says you disagree with what I said. Am I right?"

She yelled back at me, "Actually I DON'T agree with you!" Holy smokes! But remember, the big, bold, broad, generic nothing statement? Oh yeah, she had that in spades. What she didn't have was clear content. So, I responded by asking her what I had said that she disagreed with. I felt like, ball in your court now, sister!

Darn it all, she had something and she told me what it was. In that same loud and annoying way. The crazy thing was, what she disagreed with was not what I had said. She misunderstood me. I take responsibility of the effectiveness of my communication. If she misunderstood me, then I didn't explain it very well. Now I have the chance to go back and re-explain. From that point on we were on the same page. That doesn't mean she agreed with everything I said, but she would raise her hand and ask the question, and that is a beautiful thing.

I learned so much from that woman, I don't know her name, but she made an impact on me. If I had not been assertive enough to ask her and she hadn't of been assertive enough to tell me, (even though she did it aggressively) that day would have turned out very differently. She would have walked out and thought the workshop was a complete waste of time. And she was making my day miserable too! If you are looking all snarly and nasty when I am speaking, I just try not to look at you again. Those of you that smile at me and give me the periodic head nod, I like you! I will look at you again. I always say this is where my job is different than other people's jobs. For me, I come in do a workshop or keynote and leave, I don't have to see my difficult people again. You on the other hand may see them every day.

Communication matters. Speaking up matters. If we are not addressing issues as they come up, we are holding on to them. Eventually those emotions are going to blow. Remember, keeping quiet to keep the peace only keeps the tension. Speak up and resolve issues. That is making an impact.

At the end of the day, all of this—every technique, every framework, every example, it only matters if you use it. You can understand communication. You can nod your head and think, "Yes, that makes sense. I should do that." But understanding it and actually doing it are two very different things. And your impact? It lives in the doing. It lives in the moment where your heart is racing, your thoughts are loud, and everything in you wants to stay quiet, back down, or take the easy way out, and instead, you choose to lean in. You choose to speak. You choose to show up differently.

Because let's be honest, most of us already know what we should say. That's not usually the problem. The problem is that we don't say it. We hesitate. We second-guess. We overthink. We wait for the perfect time, the perfect words, and the perfect level of confidence— and in the waiting, the moment passes. The conversation doesn't happen. The idea doesn't get shared. The boundary doesn't get set. And slowly, over time, that silence starts to shape our lives in ways we didn't intend. Not because we weren't capable, but because we weren't willing to use our voice when it mattered.

And here's where I want to challenge you—because this is where everything shifts.

If your impact is your superpower, then your communication is how you activate it.

It's not optional. It's not a "nice to have."

It is the mechanism through which your ideas, your values, your boundaries, and your leadership show up in the world. And every time you choose not to communicate with intention, you are unintentionally choosing a smaller impact.

That might sound a little bold. But it's true.

Because the life you want, the relationships you want, the career you want, the respect you want, and it all requires conversations. Sometimes easy ones. Sometimes hard ones. Sometimes uncomfortable ones that you would rather avoid altogether. But avoiding them doesn't make them go away. It just delays the outcome and often makes it harder when you finally do address it.

That's why these skills matter.

Not because they make you sound smarter. Not because they make you more polished. But because they make you more effective.

When you approach communication from a results-oriented mindset, everything changes. You stop asking, "How do I say this so I don't upset anyone?" and you start asking, "How do I say this so we can actually move forward?" You stop reacting in the moment and start responding with purpose. You stop trying to "win" the conversation and start trying to solve the problem.

And that shift? That's where your impact grows.

It shows up when you choose curiosity over defensiveness. When you ask one more question instead of jumping to a conclusion. When you stay in the conversation instead of shutting it down. When you address something early instead of letting it build into something bigger than it ever needed to be.

Because here's the truth—communication is not just about expression. It's about resolution. It's about clarity. It's about connections. And ultimately, it's about ownership.

Ownership of your voice. Ownership of your message. Ownership of the role you play in every conversation you're a part of.

You don't control how other people respond. You don't control their tone, their attitude, or their level of self-awareness. But you do control how you show up. You control whether you speak or stay silent. You control whether you react or respond. You control whether you escalate or resolve.

And when you start taking ownership at that level, something really powerful happens—you stop feeling stuck.

You stop feeling like communication is something that happens to you, and you start realizing it's something you can shape. You start seeing opportunities instead of obstacles. You start recognizing that even difficult conversations can be productive, meaningful, and even relationship-building when handled with intention.

Now, does that mean it's always easy? Of course not.

There will still be moments where your voice shakes. There will still be moments where you feel intimidated, unsure, or uncomfortable. There will still be moments where that voice in your head gets loud and tries to convince you to stay quiet.

But now—you have tools. You have language. You have a way forward. And more importantly, you have a choice.

You can go back to doing what you've always done—staying quiet, avoiding discomfort, letting things build, reacting in the moment—or you can choose something different.

You can pause. You can breathe. You can ask a question. You can say the thing that needs to be said. You can use the frameworks. You can try the techniques. You can practice—imperfectly, awkwardly, and in real time.

Because that's how this works.

You don't get better at communication by reading about it. You get better by doing it. One conversation at a time. One moment at a time. One decision at a time.

And here's what I know to be true—if you will take even one of these tools and use it, if you will commit to doing just one thing differently the next time you're in a conversation that matters, you will start to see a shift. Maybe small at first. Maybe subtle. But it will build.

And over time, those small shifts become new habits. Those habits become your default. And that default becomes your impact.

Which brings us right back to where we started.

Making an impact in your life isn't about waiting until you feel ready, confident, or fearless. It's about deciding that your voice matters—even when it shakes. It's about choosing to be intentional in how you communicate, especially when it would be easier not to. It's about showing up in the moments that matter and using your voice to create clarity, connection, and progress.

Because when you do that—when you stop holding back, when you start leaning in, when you communicate with purpose—you don't just change your conversations.

You change your outcomes. You change your relationships. You change your trajectory.

And that is how you use your superpower.

No spandex suit required.

Chapter 9

Superheroes, Dolphins & Other Life Lessons

(Impact, legacy, and what really matters)

I hope you are feeling invigorated and excited and ready to jump into your own life and make an impact! I hope that as you have been reading this, you have been re-reading it, taking notes, and having more than a few "a-ha" moments. I also hope you realize it isn't about me. It is about you. It is not enough for you to read this, you must take action on it. That is the hard part.

For any of us to learn, grow, or develop, to move one step closer to our own definition of success, to make an impact, we must have two things in place. You must be willing and able.

Willing and Able

If we really want to learn, grow, and develop, if we want to define success on our own terms instead of living out someone else's version of it, then we must be both willing and able. And here's the truth most people don't talk about, being able is usually not the problem. We live in a world where information is everywhere. You can Google it, YouTube it, listen to a podcast on it, take a course on it, read a book about it. The "how" is not hard to find. The steps, the strategies, the checklists, that's the able. That's the part we tend to focus on because it feels productive. It feels safe. It feels like progress.

But the real work, the part that determines whether you actually do anything with all that knowledge, is the willing.

The willing is your self-esteem. It's your belief that you are capable, worthy, and allowed to go after what you want. It's the internal voice that either says, "Why not me?" or quietly whispers, "Who do you think you are?" And that voice matters more than any strategy ever will. Because you can have the best plan in the world, the clearest roadmap, the most step-by-step process imaginable, but if you don't believe you can execute it, you won't. Not fully. Not consistently. Not in a way that creates real change.

Think about how this shows up.

You might know exactly how to ask for a promotion. You've read the articles. You've practiced the conversation. You've even written down your talking points. That's the able. But when the moment comes, if your self-talk sounds like, "They're probably going to say no," or "I'm not as qualified as everyone else," or "I should just be grateful I have a job" you hesitate. You soften your ask. You talk yourself out of it entirely. The opportunity doesn't disappear because you weren't able. It disappears because you weren't willing.

Or maybe it's something more personal. You know how to set boundaries. You've heard it a hundred times, say no, protect your time, and communicate clearly. But when someone asks for something that stretches you too thin, your immediate thought isn't, "What do I need?" It's, "I don't want to disappoint them." So you say yes. Again. Not because you don't know how to say no, but because somewhere deep down, you've tied your value to being agreeable, helpful, and accommodating. That's not a skills issue. That's a self-esteem issue.

The willing is what determines whether you apply the able.

And this is where so many people get stuck. They keep trying to gather more information, more tools, more techniques, thinking that the next strategy will be the thing that finally moves them forward. But what they actually need is not more instruction. They need more belief. They need to strengthen the part of them that says, "I can do this," and just as importantly, "I deserve to."

Because here's the reality: growth requires discomfort. It requires you to do things before you feel fully ready. It requires you to risk being wrong, being seen, being judged, or even failing. And if your self-esteem isn't strong enough to support you through that discomfort, you will default back to what feels safe, even if what feels safe is what's keeping you stuck.

Being willing doesn't mean you're fearless. It means you're choosing to move forward anyway.

It's raising your hand even when your voice shakes.

It's having the conversation even when you're unsure how it will go.

It's taking the step even when you don't have the entire path figured out.

And every time you do that, every time you act in a way that aligns with the person you want to become, you strengthen your self-esteem. You build evidence. You prove to yourself, "I can handle this."

That's how willing grows.

I think of it as more than self-esteem. It is three pieces: the self-ideal, the self-image, and the self-esteem.

The self-ideal is you at your best self. It is the ideal you that you picture in your mind's eye. You at your best self! How you see yourself in an ideal world.

Your self-image is how you see yourself behaving on a daily basis.

Your self-esteem is the difference between the two.

This is how I think about it. If myself ideal, the way I ideally see myself in my mind, my best version of me is that I lead a healthy lifestyle. I make healthy choices and eat healthy. That is my ideal self. Then for lunch I go through a drive through and order a burger, after I eat that burger I feel terrible. I beat myself up for it and my inner voice is going into overdrive telling me how bad I am. I feel guilty and disappointed. My self-image did not live up to myself ideal so my self-esteem goes down. On the other hand, if myself ideal is me making healthy food choices and for lunch I eat a big salad, I feel great! I am proud of myself and my self-esteem goes up! And clearly, I get to have ice cream for dessert, right? The self-esteem is the difference between yourself ideal and your self-image.

It works the same in all areas of our life. Think about it at work. If your self-ideal is you stand up for yourself, you speak up when you have ideas and questions and you never let anyone step on you or take advantage of you. So, in a meeting, your co-worker, we will call him Jim. Jim makes a rude comment to you or says your idea needs work in a less than kind way and you are steaming mad. Your self-ideal would dictate that you speak up, you challenge Jim, in a professional and tactful way of course, but you say something. When you see yourself doing that, your self-image confirms yourself ideal and your self-esteem goes up. Think about how you feel about yourself after that interaction? Even if it doesn't go exactly the way you wanted, you still feel good for speaking up. However, if you do not say anything, you stay quiet and let Jim walk all over you, and your self-image does not live up to yourself ideal and your self-esteem goes down.

Our self esteem is rooted in our behavior. Our behavior is our able.

So yes, we need the able. We need the tools, the techniques, the strategies. But without the willing, they sit unused. They stay theoretical. They become things we "know" but never actually live.

If you want to make a real impact, create real change, if you want to define success for yourself and actually go after it, you have to work on both.

You have to build the skills.

And you have to build the belief.

Because when those two things come together, that is the magic.

That's when you stop wishing for change...and start creating it. And trust me when I tell you, you have the power. You have the power to be more, do more, and make more of an impact on your life and the lives around you!

Years and years ago, (I don't even want to try and count how many!) I was in my early twenties and had recently moved to Texas. I was searching for where I fit in and where my life was headed. I knew I was destined for something bigger and better but man, oh man, I had no idea what that was going to be. My Mom had started her own business and found great success. She was amazing! I saw how hard she worked and the hours she put in and I also saw how rewarding it was. I am truly blessed that she was there to guide me. She was attending a luncheon event with a keynote speaker, and she invited me to join her. I had never really done anything like that before, but I was all in for that free lunch!

The speaker's name was Mamie McCullough. I will never forget her! She was funny, and interesting, and she told great stories! And she was very southern! Her accent was such a huge part of who she was and how she told stories and she mesmerized me. I even bought her cassette tape! (Yes, that is how old I am. If you are younger and you are reading this, feel free to ask a Gen Xer what a cassette tape is!)

Over the years the cassette disappeared, and a lot of her message from that day is fuzzy but there is one thing she said that I will never forget. She told us all to look at our thumbs, check out our thumbprint, and she reminded us that everyone has a unique and individual thumbprint. And that is God's reminder that you are thumb-body! Say it out loud for the full effect, trust me. And you ARE thumb-body! You are a unique and special child of God, and you have been given very special gifts. The thing about gifts though, is that for them to truly be a gift, you must give them away.

You must be willing and able to give that gift away. Which one do you need to focus on right now in your life to make that impact we are talking about? What do you need to start with? Think about it and take that step. You can do it, because you are thumb-body!

For us to show up differently at work, to grow, to develop, to be better, to make a bigger impact on our lives and the lives of those around us, we have to embrace hard things.

That is the Dojo.

When you're doing new stuff, when you're learning, you're growing, you're in the dojo. The dojo is, of course, a Japanese word or concept. In English, it basically means the place of the way. It's the training ground. The dojo is when you are "in between." It's the space, it's the energy between where you are now and where you want to be. That's the dojo. It's the training ground.

To get from where you are to where you want to be you have to make it through the dojo. We talked in an earlier chapter about the importance of resilience, so if you need to go back and re-read that go for it! Because resilience is a key to getting through the dojo. Remember what I said before, one of the greatest lessons I have learned is that hard is not a sign you're on the wrong path. Hard is the path.

And the first day in the dojo is usually pretty easy! Let's say, you made the decision to get healthy. You are going to eat healthier, exercise, and just make better lifestyle choices. And you are committed! On day one. You go to work, and someone brings donuts. And you quickly and convincingly say no, thank you! You don't want donuts; you are choosing a healthy lifestyle! You are not even tempted. You are in the dojo.

Then the day happens. The stress, the overwhelm, you have to work late, the project timeline is changed...again. The kids need picking up, there's a baseball game for your son, they need dinner and help with homework. And is that laundry pile really that big? You are exhausted and overwhelmed. And then day two in the dojo. Who brought in donuts...again!? Well, maybe just eating one donut isn't that bad? Day two in the dojo is always harder.

The key to the dojo, you have to have the courage to enter and the resilience to stay.

That's the able part of the willing and able. If you expect to get through that dojo and achieve that goal, make that impact, make that positive change in your life, what are you going to do differently? How are you going to step into that arena and make the change? And you have to have the courage to do it. You gotta get in that dojo!

President Theodore Roosevelt is known for his "Man in the Arena" quote. The famous "Man in the Arena" quote is a passage from Theodore Roosevelt's 1910 speech "Citizenship in the Republic," delivered at the Sorbonne in Paris. It emphasizes that credit belongs to those who strive, fail, and act, rather than the critics.

Theodore Roosevelt said, "It is not the critic who counts; not the man who points out how the strong man stumbles, or where the doer of deeds could have done them better. The credit belongs to the man who is actually in the arena, whose face is marred by dust and sweat and blood; who strives valiantly; who errs, who comes short again and again, because there is no effort without error and shortcoming; but who does actually strive to do the deeds; who knows great enthusiasms, the great devotions; who spends himself in a worthy cause; who at the best knows in the end the triumph of high achievement, and who at the worst, if he fails, at least fails while daring greatly, so that his place shall never be with those cold and timid souls who neither know victory nor defeat."

The arena is like the dojo. It generally requires daring greatly, and essentially, betting on yourself. I believe in you. Do you believe in you?

Once you enter the dojo, you must stay there until it is finished. No matter what. No matter what life throws at you.

That's recognizing day two of the donuts. It's easy to say no the first day. The grit happens on day two, day three, day four, day 54, day 104. Anybody that exercises understand this. Not that I have always understood that! I have had more than one occasion in my life when I went to the gym, got in a little workout, and then was annoyed the next day when I didn't look ten pounds thinner. I mean, geez. I went to the gym for pete's sake! Why didn't it work?

We all know it is not about what you do once. It is about what you do consistently.

That means, no matter what happens around you, no matter what life throws at you, you must be consistent. That is what sets people apart. Anyone can do it once. Not everyone can do it consistently. It doesn't matter what kind of bullshit that is happening around you, you do it anyway!

Doing it when it is easy is not special. It is not the behavior of a high achiever.

I see this concept in action even in areas you might not expect. Even in customer service. I have taught a ton of customer service classes over the years. I have always laughed when people say they think they are great at customer service, if the customers are nice. When the customers get mad or mean, then they get mad and mean back! If you are only good at customer service when the people are nice, you aren't great at service, you aren't even mediocre! What makes you great is doing it even when the customer isn't great. It is in spite of the customer's attitude. They don't change your attitude, you change theirs.

You can't let the circumstances, the drama, the things that are going to get thrown at you every day break you. I love that line from Rocky 4. (I told y'all I was a Sylvester Stallone fan, right?)

In the final fight of the movie, when Rocky is taking on Ivan Drago the big guy from Russia that killed Apollo Creed, and Drago looks at Rocky and says, "I must break you." Holy cow! It gives me chills every time! Nobody or nothing can break you unless you let it!

Nobody gets to break you. And next time something gets thrown at you, I want you to put your Rocky boxing gloves on and fight. I know it's mixing Rocky movies, but y'all remember Rocky 3 when Rocky fought Clubber Lang? He says, "I'm gonna bust you up!" Do you remember what Rocky said? He said, "Go for it!" That is what I want you to say the next time it feels like someone or something is trying to break you, your response, in true Rocky fashion, is going to be, "Go for it!"

Remember, Rocky was never really about winning. What did he always say? It was about going the distance. That's the dojo. I think I have proven that everything you need to know about life you can learn from Rocky movies!

It doesn't matter what's thrown at you. We don't only do right when things are going well. Everyone reading this, yes, you. You are powerful. Every one of you bring your own strength, your own talent to the table. Every one of you has your own gift.

So you have to see yourself as your own superhero! Trust me, it's true.

One of the strangest things about human beings is this: we can spot greatness in everyone else from a mile away but somehow become legally blind when it comes to ourselves.

We will cheer for our friends, brag on our kids, encourage our coworkers, and hype up complete strangers on social media like we're their full-time public relations team. We will tell other people they are talented, capable, smart, strong, creative, inspiring, and important. But when it comes to our own gifts? Suddenly we act like we are applying for undercover witness protection.

"Oh, it was nothing."

"Anybody could've done it."

"I'm not really that special."

"I just got lucky."

No ma'am. Sit down. We need to talk.

Why are you so quick to dismiss the very things that make you valuable? Why are you so comfortable minimizing your impact? Why do you speak about yourself with a level of criticism you would never use on someone you love?

Somewhere along the way, many of us learned that shrinking ourselves was the polite thing to do. We learned to stay quiet, not take up too much space, not sound "too confident," not draw attention to ourselves, and certainly not acknowledge our own strengths out loud. We became experts at celebrating everyone else while quietly disqualifying ourselves.

And let me lovingly call this behavior out for what it is: self-abdication.

You are handing away ownership of your worth while simultaneously wondering why you feel unseen.

Here's the truth: the people around you are already benefiting from your value every single day, even if you refuse to acknowledge it. Your family feels your impact. Your children are shaped by your presence, your words, your sacrifices, and your love. Your workplace is influenced by your ideas, your work ethic, your energy, and your leadership. Your friends lean on your wisdom, your humor, your encouragement, and your strength. Your community benefits from your compassion and your willingness to show up when it matters.

You matter more than you think you do.

And yet so many people walk through life acting as if their role is "background character with snacks." And if you know me, you know I do love me some snacks!

So. Let me lovingly kick you in the mindset again. Girl... why are you acting like you are the unpaid intern in your own life?

You will praise up Brenda from accounting for remembering to attach a stupid PDF, but someone compliments you and suddenly you're out here acting like a fugitive from praise.

Meanwhile, you're over here acting like your contributions are just decorative throw pillows. You were not created to disappear into the wallpaper of your own life.

The problem is not that you lack value. The problem is that you have become so accustomed to discounting yourself that you no longer recognize the weight of your contribution. You have normalized minimizing your brilliance. You have confused humility with invisibility.

Those are not the same thing.

Being humble does not require pretending you are powerless. It does not require denying your gifts, dismissing your accomplishments, or silencing your voice. In fact, refusing to acknowledge your strengths helps no one. The world does not benefit when capable, compassionate, gifted people spend their lives hiding in the shadows waiting for permission to matter.

And can we be honest about something else? Sometimes we keep ourselves small because small feels safe. If we do not fully step into our gifts, then we do not risk failure, criticism, rejection, or responsibility. Playing small gives us an escape hatch. But it also keeps us from fully showing up in the lives we were meant to live.

You cannot create impact while constantly apologizing for your existence.

At some point, you have to decide that hiding is no longer serving you.

The truth is, you already are influencing people every single day. The question is not whether you have impact. The question is whether you are intentionally using it. Whether you are owning it. Whether you are willing to stop shrinking long enough to let your light shine the way it was always meant to.

Maybe sometimes you forget that God very clearly tells us in the Bible that you are the salt and the light.

Matthew Chapter 5 verses 13-16.

Salt and Light

You are the salt of the earth. But if the salt loses its saltiness, how can it be made salty again? It is no longer good for anything, except to be thrown out and trampled underfoot.

You are the light of the world. A town built on a hill cannot be hidden. Neither do people light a lamp and put it under a bowl. Instead, they put it on its stand, and it gives light to everyone in the house. In the same way, let your light shine before others so that they may see your good deeds and glorify your Father in heaven.

I think God has got us here, don't you?

Not watered-down, dimmed-down, exhausted-from-carrying-everyone-else light. Real light. The kind that changes rooms when it walks in. The kind that gives hope, direction, courage, and warmth to the people around you.

Salt because you, yes, YOU spice up the world. Just like some good Himalayan sea salt makes a steak irresistible, you make the world a more flavorful and richer place. Just by being in it. So, learn to throw that saltiness around like confetti! Be salty, man, just be salty! (Great. Now, I am hungry for a steak...)

And maybe it is finally time you stopped waiting for someone else to tell you that you do in fact matter. Maybe it is time to believe it yourself. Because you cannot create impact while constantly apologizing for your existence.

Smells Like Imposter Syndrome to Me.

I have always found the phrase Impostor Syndrome interesting because it sounds so permanent. So official. So clinical. Like you have been diagnosed with a lifelong condition and now you're doomed to wander through conference rooms and staff meetings forever whispering, "I don't belong here," while clutching an iced coffee and pretending to understand Excel pivot tables.

But what if it is not a syndrome at all?

What if it is just a really bad habit of self-dismissal and self-abdication?

What if it is years of talking yourself out of your own value? Years of minimizing your gifts, shrinking your voice, dismissing your accomplishments, and giving everyone else credit while treating your own contributions like they were accidental?

Because let's be honest: most people struggling with so-called imposter syndrome are not actually imposters. They are usually some of the most capable, responsible, over prepared people in the room. These are the people showing up early, staying late, double-checking everything, carrying entire teams emotionally, remembering birthdays, solving problems nobody else wanted to touch, or just plain saving the day, time after time, and yet somehow still believing they are one typo away from being exposed as frauds.

Meanwhile, Chad in the next office has confidence levels so high they should honestly be studied by science.

That is the disconnect.

The people doubting themselves are often the very people creating the most impact.

I think we need a better name for this phenomenon. "Imposter syndrome" sounds like something you catch. I think a more accurate name would be "cape hiding." Because that is what so many people are doing? They are hiding their strengths, downplaying their brilliance, and acting like their gifts are somehow less valuable than everyone else's. But the superhero cape is there. You just have to learn to let it fly!

And can we talk about how ridiculous we become when someone compliments us?

Someone says, "You did an amazing job on that presentation," and immediately we respond with: "I just threw it together." Or "I got lucky." Or "It was a team effort."

Now listen. There is absolutely nothing wrong with humility and teamwork. But some of y'all reject compliments so aggressively that people practically need emotional shin guards to encourage you.

At some point, it stops being humility and starts becoming self-erasure.

You would never speak to your best friend the way you speak to yourself. If your friend got promoted, landed a client, built a business, survived a hard season, raised amazing kids, or finally found the courage to use their voice, you would be cheering for them like they just won an Olympic medal. But when you accomplish something? Suddenly you become a part-time historian whose only job is documenting every flaw, mistake, insecurity, and awkward moment from 2007. And if you are like a lot of us, it keeps you up at night.

It is exhausting.

And the truth is, when you constantly minimize yourself, you do not just hurt yourself, you rob the people around you too. Your family needs your confidence. Your team needs your ideas. Your workplace needs your leadership. Your children need to see what it looks like for someone to own their value without apology. The world does not benefit when good people spend their lives hiding in the emotional witness protection program.

Maybe the goal is not to "overcome imposter syndrome."

Maybe the goal is to stop arguing with the evidence of your own life. And you have the receipts. You do have a record of success.

You are not an imposter because you are still growing. You are not a fraud because you do not know everything. You are not disqualified because you feel nervous. Growth feels uncomfortable sometimes. Leadership feels uncomfortable sometimes. Visibility feels uncomfortable sometimes. But discomfort is not proof you do not belong.

Sometimes it is proof you are finally stepping into the room you were meant for.

One of the biggest lies we tell ourselves is that the loudest voice in our lives is coming from other people. Most of the time, it is not. The loudest voice is the one living inside our own head. The running commentary. The internal critic. The tiny emotional internet troll that apparently signed a long-term lease in our brain and refuses to leave.

You know the voice I'm talking about.

The one that whispers things like:

"Don't speak up. You'll sound stupid."

"Who do you think you are?"

"You're not qualified enough."

"Someone else could do this better."

And let's face that internet troll voice loves to run through every mistake you made in high school at 2:00 AM. Lying in bed when all you desperately want is to fall asleep! That voice you hear when you are staring at the ceiling and thinking that you will never recover from the traumatic day in eighth grade when you were walking to the front of the class to give that oral book report with your dress stuck in your pantyhose. And the voice in your head is naming every person that saw it and every person they told and how they all still talk about it today! And you convince yourself that even though it was 25 years ago, they probably still have big reunion parties where they talk only about you! Whew. That was exhausting. And ridiculous. Why do we torture ourselves like that? Knock it off.

First of all, that voice is dramatic. Second, it is wildly inconsistent. Somehow it has convinced many people that they are responsible for everything, should carry everyone else emotionally, must solve every problem, and keep the entire world spinning... while simultaneously believing they have little value themselves.

Make that make sense.

So much of what we call Impostor Syndrome is not actually about lack of ability. It is about years of absorbed messages that taught us to doubt ourselves. Criticism. Rejection. Comparison. Perfectionism. Toxic workplaces. Unhealthy relationships. Being underestimated. Being told to stay quiet, stay agreeable, stay humble, and stay small. Over time, those outside voices become internal ones, and eventually we stop questioning them altogether. We just accept them as truth.

That is the dangerous part.

Because your brain will repeat what it hears most often—even when it is wrong?

Some people have spent so much time rehearsing their flaws that they can no longer see their strengths clearly. They remember every awkward moment, every failure, every criticism, every mistake, every opportunity they missed. Meanwhile, they completely overlook the evidence of their own impact. The people they helped. The problems they solved. The hard seasons they survived. The courage it took to keep going when life was heavy. The moments they showed up when it mattered most.

It is amazing to me how many capable, intelligent, compassionate people walk through life acting like unpaid interns in their own story.

You will cheer for everybody else. You will hype up your friends, encourage your coworkers, support your spouse, celebrate your children, and clap the loudest for people you care about. But when someone compliments you? Suddenly you turn into a defensive attorney arguing against your own value.

"You did such a great job!" "Oh, it was nothing." "I just got lucky." "Anybody could've done it."

No. They couldn't. That is why you did it.

At some point, we need to lovingly call this behavior out for what it is: self-erasure disguised as humility.

Real humility does not require you to pretend you are powerless. It does not require you to deny your gifts, shrink your voice, or downplay your impact. In fact, constantly dismissing yourself helps no one. The world does not benefit when gifted, compassionate, capable people spend their entire lives hiding behind insecurity and apologizing for taking up space.

And honestly, some of you would never tolerate another person speaking to your children the way you speak to yourselves internally. If someone followed your child around all day whispering: "You're not good enough." "You'll probably fail." "Nobody cares what you think." "You should just stay quiet." —you would absolutely lose your mind. If anyone said anything like that to one of my precious perfect nieces, well, let's just say someone would need to get me some bail money. Because that would never be allowed! Some of y'all would end up on the evening news over less. Yet internally, many people allow that same destructive voice to narrate their entire lives unchecked.

At some point, you have to stop automatically agreeing with every cruel thought that enters your mind. Not every insecurity deserves authority. Not every fear is telling the truth. Not every thought deserves a microphone.

And maybe confidence is not becoming the loudest person in the room. Maybe confidence is finally learning to stop arguing with the evidence of your own life. Maybe it is recognizing that discomfort does not mean you are unqualified. It does not mean you are an imposter. Sometimes discomfort is simply proof that you are growing into a bigger version of yourself.

You are not an imposter because you are still learning. You are not a fraud because you feel nervous. You are not disqualified because you do not have everything figured out.

You are human.

And maybe it is finally time to take off the oversized coat of self-doubt that never really fit you in the first place. And let that superhero cape fly high!

I want this book to be relatable, so if you are thinking, "Wow... that's me." Good. Now you know where you need to work. So the next step is, what do you DO about it?

I like to think my approach is grounded and practical because you do not need another fluffy "just love yourself!" speech while they are actively spiraling in a Target parking lot questioning their entire existence. Can I get an Amen, there?

What you need are tangible ways to interrupt the pattern.

Start by embracing this. (Sort of a mic drop moment if I do say so myself!)

You do not overcome imposter syndrome by becoming perfect.

You overcome it by changing your relationship with your own thoughts.

I will share some of the things I have spent time working on that have helped me but remember it is about the action you take and DO that will make the difference, not the things you read about. I mean think about it... reading about a fabulous trip to Maui is not the same as getting on that plane and putting those toes in the sand with an adult beverage in your hand! Maybe that is just me.

One of the first ways we begin overcoming negative self-talk is by recognizing that not every thought deserves immediate belief. Some people treat every insecurity like it arrived via certified mail directly from the universe. Trust me, it did not.

Sometimes a thought is just a thought. Sometimes it is fear. Sometimes it is old conditioning. Sometimes it is exhaustion, rejection, insecurity, comparison, burnout, or years of carrying around criticism that was never yours to keep in the first place.

You must learn to challenge the voice instead of automatically surrendering to it.

Another huge step is learning to separate humility from self-erasure.

There is a difference between being grounded and constantly minimizing yourself. Healthy confidence says: "I do not know everything, but I bring value."

Meanwhile, imposter syndrome says: "If I am not perfect, I must be worthless."

That is not humility. That is emotional sabotage wearing sensible shoes.

You need to stop collecting evidence only for their failures.

Some of y'all keep detailed emotional archives of every awkward thing you have ever said since 1988, but somehow forget every success, breakthrough, compliment, solved problem, and meaningful contribution you have ever made. Your brain becomes what you repeatedly rehearse. If you constantly replay your failures, your confidence never stands a chance. Write a list of your accomplishments, big and small, and use that file to go back to when you are feeling "less than."

Another important step is taking action before you feel fully confident.

This one makes people mad because everybody wants confidence to arrive first like a motivational Amazon Prime delivery.

Usually it does not.

Confidence is built through action, not before it. Most impactful people are not fearless. They are simply willing to move while nervous. We talked a lot about this in another chapter. Resilience is a key skill for impact makers.

And honestly? One of the healthiest things you can do is pay attention to whose voices you have allowed to live rent free in your head.

Some people are still living under the weight of a teacher's criticism, a parent's disappointment, a toxic boss, a bad relationship, comparison, rejection, or somebody who underestimated those years ago.

Meanwhile, the person who said those things has moved on with their life, and you are still carrying their words around like emotional carry-on luggage, and that overhead bin is full.

At some point, you have to decide whose opinion actually deserves authority in your life.

The last thing I want you to try is this. Every time you catch yourself saying something negative to yourself about not being smart enough, educated enough, pretty enough, whatever your negative voice is saying to you. I want you to stop right there. And I want you to picture someone saying it to your daughter instead of you. Or your niece. Or your granddaughter, or son, or nephew, whoever is the younger person in your life that you love the most. If it's not OK to say it to them then it's not OK to say it to you. Lead by example.

You would never tell your best friend:

"Don't even try."

"You'll embarrass yourself."

"You probably are not capable."

But internally? Some people say those things to themselves daily.

The goal is not arrogance. The goal is alignment. Speaking to yourself in a way that is truthful, healthy, encouraging, and grounded instead of constantly destructive.

The voice in your head becomes the soundtrack of your life.

Make sure it is not narrating you into a smaller future.

Because remember, you have to be your own superhero!

Superheroes

When I tell people they are a superhero that generally don't believe me. Unless of course they have an invisible jet, a truth lasso, a utility belt and a cape, which never seems to happen.

Let's approach this from a different angle. I want you to do this exercise. And I mean really do it. I prefer that you do this on paper not in your head, I really want you to see the results. So if you need to stop and pause between steps, take all the time you need.

First, write down the name of someone you think of as a personal hero to you. Someone you look up to and admire. They can be someone you know personally, a family member or a friend, someone you know professionally, or someone from history, or even a celebrity. Write down their name.

Now, I want you to look at that name and write down three to five traits or characteristics about that person that you most admire. I want to be clear here, traits or characteristics, not accomplishments.

For example, let's say you wrote down Oprah. (I get that one a lot!) You can't write down that you admire how she was poor and now she is rich. That is an accomplishment. What you might write down instead is that she had a lot of courage and perseverance to do what she did. What specific traits does this person possess? It could be confidence, or compassion, or being a great listener, cared deeply about people, always stayed positive no matter the circumstances, or never complained. Those are all powerful traits. Just remember, there are a million different ones, so what are the ones you associate with your hero person?

Take a little time if you need to. For some people this comes quickly, for others you really need to marinate in it. So, stop reading until you have done these two steps.

(Hear the Jeopardy music playing in the background?)

So glad you took the time to do this and came back to it.

Although I don't know who you wrote down and what traits you admire, I can share a few that I hear most often. I hear Mother Teresa quite a bit. Taylor Swift has been more times than I would have thought possible, bosses, grandparents, and dads get mentioned. I will tell you though, in all of the years I have had people do this exercise, the number one answer I hear is Mom. Mom gets a lot of love!

The traits I hear tend to be things like they are empathetic, compassionate, spiritual, loyal, forgiving, positive attitude makes the list a lot. Maybe you wrote something like this or maybe you came up with something totally different.

Here is what I want you to hear. Psychologists tell us, the traits and characteristics you most admire in others, are the traits and characteristics you, yourself possess. Believe it or not, you just described yourself!

When I tell people that the common response tends to be things like, no not me, I wish, that would be nice, but YES, YOU. Yes, you. Maybe they aren't as transparent, maybe they need to be worked on and developed. But they are there. Sometimes it is hard for us to see our own superpowers!

Hank's Deer Story

It's hard for us to see that value. Maybe it's just one of those things we have to kind of dig in a little more on. I always tell people that I actually learned this from my husband. I describe my husband as my rugged outdoorsman. He is a retired firefighter, paramedic, He flew for care flight. He was an RN. And he's the outdoorsy guy. He's the hunter, the fisherman, the camper, he does all the things, and I just adore my husband. And when I moved from California and I moved to Texas, I was confirmed single, y'all. I had no intention of getting married, I wasn't looking for a spouse, I hardly even dated. I wasn't against it; I just was really focused on my career at the point.

I was so focused on what I was doing in my career that dating was just not on my radar. As a matter of fact, when I went out on my 1st date with my now husband, my mom and sister made a bet about whether or not I would cancel. My mom called every guy I dated, Brad. She called my husband, Brad, for the first 2 months that we dated, because she figured, why bother to get to know his name, I am just going to dump him anyway. That's a true story. One day my soon to be husband asked me, "Did your Mom just call me Brad?" I laughed out loud and told him to just roll with it. His name's Hank, by the way.

When I first met him though, I didn't know what it was, but I knew pretty quickly that I was smitten. I just knew he was the one. Apparently way before he knew, but that is another story! Anyway, we hadn't been dating that long, and my rugged outdoorsman tells me he wants to take me deer scouting. I don't know if y'all know what that is. I had no idea what that was, he had to explain it to me. If you don't know, deer scouting is basically where you go out, you hike around the woods, and you look for where the deer might be. That's it. You look for where the deer might be. I guess they are gathering vital data for when deer season hits so they know all the deer in the neighborhood. Makes for a good hunt.

When he asked me to go and told me what it was, what I heard was hiking! Hiking means new boots! Yay! I am in. I know this would be so much fun. So I get up at the crack of dawn (Apparently this is when the deer scouting is supposed to occur. He failed to mention that when he asked me originally. But I got to put my cute new boots on and we headed to the woods. We went up north of the Dallas area where we live to an area around Lake Texoma. It is so beautiful there the woods and the trees, it's just stunning!

We leave at the crack of dawn and drive up there as soon as he parks the truck, we are starting our deer scout. I am just so excited! So, I keep asking him, "Where are the deer? I don't see any deer? Where are the deer?" Over and over again, I ask and over and over again he keeps responding, "Sssshhhh. You have to be quiet, or it will scare them away." I realized at that point in our adventure, that this particular hobby may not be very well suited to my personality style.

He kept telling me to be quiet. He said, "Shh, you have to be quiet." But I would say I don't see any deer! Then he would tell me that I had to dig deeper. Just because I didn't see them at first didn't mean they weren't there. I had to be patient. I just kept telling him I wanted to see deer. Then, when he said to dig deeper, just because you don't see them at first doesn't mean they are there, he started to show me all the signs the deer were there. He could pick out all the hoof prints in the ground, tell me how many there were, which way they were heading and what size they were. It was amazing! He showed me all the rubbings on trees where the deer had rubbed their antlers. And he would say again, "See, they are here. You just have to be patient. Just because you don't see them at first, doesn't mean they are there. Be patient."

We hiked and hiked for hours. And all day, I never saw one stinking deer, not one. I was convinced I would never see any deer doing it like that.

That night, we slept in a tent by the lake. Mind you, this was the very first time I'd ever slept in a tent on the ground. Did I mention we were on the ground? It was a tent on the ground with no air mattress, just a blanket. It was cozy. If you've ever slept in a tent on the ground, then you know, you wake up at the crack of dawn because you're sleeping on the ground in a tent. Would have been cozier if I had a younger back. At the crack of dawn I wake up and I unzip the tent just enough that I can look outside. And oh my stars, it was beautiful!

It was absolutely amazing. The bright orange sun was just coming up over the lake, making the reflection of the lake look like glass, it sparkled! It was gorgeous. The lake is surrounded by all these towering beautiful trees. As I look around and I am just taking it all in, I spot it. Off to the left there is a patch of grass right on the edge of the lake under some of those trees. And standing there looking right at me—was a whole bunch of deer! Big ones, little ones, some of the deer I swear were looking me dead in the eye and others seemed oblivious to my presence. It was so spectacular! I started shaking my husband to wake him up. How he was able to sleep through all that is still a mystery! But I said, "look! Deer!" He chuckled to himself, not sure if he thought I was cute or clueless, or both. But he told me again. I told you they are here. Just because you don't see them at first doesn't mean they aren't there, you have to be patient.

Yeah, he taught me that. And that is what I want to teach you. Those traits and characteristics you wrote down? Yes they are you. Sometimes you must be a little patient with yourself. And sometimes, just because you don't see them first, doesn't mean they're not there. You might need to dig a little deeper. Because all the signs are there. Keep looking for and acknowledge the evidence, I promise you it's there. Keep digging, keep growing, keep learning, keep taking ownership of self. Because when you do, you will see it too. You have superpowers.

You are like electricity. Think about it. The life you want is right here, it's right in front of you, right now. It's like electricity. Before the invention of the light bulb, most people weren't aware electricity even existed. It was still here of course, even in the same way it is here now. But we had not yet discovered it. It took the invention of the light bulb to bring it to our attention. We had to understand how to manifest it into our own reality. Think of the hero exercise as a way you just manifested those traits, those superpowers, into your reality. And now that you know it is there, imagine what you can accomplish!

This is the Hokey Pokey.

This is the hokey pokey. Because this is what it's all about? Making an impact on your life is critical. But it is bigger than that. It is about making an impact on those around you. Your family, friends, coworkers, employees, bosses, your community. You are a leader and you want to lead with impact. It was never just about you. Your destiny is bigger. See, if you have a gift, the only way it can be a true gift is if you give it away. That's why singers must sing and painters must paint, because when God gives you talents and gifts he wants you to share them. Impact isn't just for our glory, it is for those we love.

Now you get to take back control and decide, how do you want to show up for work? How do you want to show up in your personal life? What kind of wake are you leaving?

Here is what I mean.

One of my favorite places on a cruise ship is the very back of the boat. Not the buffet, or the bar, which is shocking considering my relationship with chardonnay. Ok, the bar is a close second. Not even the casino. Not even the pool deck with tiny umbrella drinks and people aggressively relaxing. Nope. I love standing at the back of the ship staring at the wake stretching out behind us for miles.

There is just something mesmerizing about it.

This gigantic ship cuts through the ocean leaving evidence everywhere it goes. The water cannot interact with that ship and stay unchanged. There is movement. Impact. A trail. Proof that something powerful passed through.

And honestly? People are exactly the same way.

Every single one of us is leaving a wake behind us everywhere we go. At work. At home. In meetings. In marriages. In friendships. In traffic. In group texts. In the school pickup line where everybody is one inconvenience away from a complete emotional collapse.

You are leaving an imprint on the people around you whether you realize it or not.

The question is not:

"Am I making an impact?"

Oh, you are.

The real question is:

"What kind of wake am I leaving behind me?"

Because some people leave encouragement, laughter, calm, confidence, safety, and strength behind them. And other people leave emotional debris and unresolved tension like a human tornado in leggings.

Some people walk into a room, and everybody relaxes.

Other people walk into a room, and everybody suddenly needs a support animal.

That is impact.

And here is what I think is important: making an impact is not about ego. It is not about applause, attention, followers, or becoming the star of your own motivational documentary. Real impact is about influence. It is about understanding that your attitude, your words, your reactions, your energy, and your behavior affect people every single day.

You are leaving a wake regardless.

You might as well make it intentional.

I think people hear the word "leader" and immediately imagine some executive standing on a stage with a headset microphone saying things like,

"Let's circle back and synergize." But leadership is so much bigger than job titles. We are all leading somewhere. We are all influencing someone.

Your kids are watching you.

Your coworkers are watching you.

Your team is watching you.

Your spouse is watching you.

The barista at Starbucks has probably seen enough to write a documentary about your stress levels.

People learn from how you show up.

They learn from how you handle pressure. How you speak to people. How you respond when things go sideways. How you treat others when you are tired, frustrated, overwhelmed, or running on caffeine and blind optimism.

That is leadership.

And can I lovingly call something out for a second? Some people are out here giving their best energy to strangers and coworkers all day long... then coming home acting like the final emotionally unstable contestant on a reality survival show.

At work:

"Absolutely! Happy to help! Great job, everyone!"

At home:

"WHY ARE THERE SHOES IN THE MIDDLE OF THE FLOOR AGAIN?!"

Listen. We have all been there. But it matters because the wake we leave at home counts too. Actually, it probably counts the most.

Our impact is not measured only in the big public moments where everybody is clapping for us. It is measured in ordinary moments. In our tone. Our patience. Our encouragement. Our consistency. The way people feel after interacting with us.

Do people feel stronger after being around you?

Safer? More confident? More seen? More valued?

Or do they feel criticized, dismissed, ignored, or emotionally exhausted?

Because here is the truth: people may forget your exact words, but they will absolutely remember the wake you left behind.

They will remember how you made them feel.

They will remember whether your presence brought light or stress.

Whether you built people up or tore them down.

Whether you showed up with grace—or just weird vibes and a lot of unresolved issues.

And maybe that is the real power of impact.

Not perfection.

Not fame.

Not being the loudest person in the room.

Just choosing, day after day, to leave behind courage, kindness, honesty, laughter, strength, accountability, and light everywhere your life touches.

Because long after the ship passes, the water still remembers it was there.

The bottom line is, this sounds a lot like your responsibility. I am not responsible for what you do with this information, you are. Reading it is great! (Really it is! Recommend the book to everyone you know!) Feeling encouraged or equipped is great. I surely hope that is how you are feeling. But again, it is your responsibility to take action on what you have read. And action can be scary. Taking risks is hard.

Dolphins

I have the most amazing sister in the world. She is the most beautiful, smart, compassionate, giving, and ridiculously funny person I know. She is that sister, that perfect sister. She is my best friend. We take sister trips and do sister dinners and we go to Elvis Tribute Artist shows and to Graceland we text each other silly memes and video all day and have entire conversations just using movie quotes.

She is my baby sister, I am seven years older than her, and I have loved her since the day my Mom told me she was having a baby! From the day she was born she was like a child for me, I became her second Mom. We have always been so close, to this day we are truly best friends.

When my sister was little, maybe six years old or so, my Mom enrolled her in swimming lessons, and my sister loved it. She was a fish immediately, she was just a natural in the water. At the end of her swim school year all the kids had a little graduation ceremony. And y'all imagine it, I mean, these little kids are, six, seven, eight years old. They're all in their bathing suits, and they have on these little graduation caps, and they got to go up on these risers at the end of the pool and get their little diplomas. It was adorable.

My sister was the only one in the whole school that got the highest award. She got a dolphin diploma. Oh, man, that was the big time! She was so excited and from that moment on, she loved dolphins! Everything dolphins and everywhere dolphins. She even became a Miami Dolphins football fan. She loved Dan Marino! (And still does!) Y'all remember back in the day, they had the Sears Wish Book Catalog that came out at Christmas? And they would sell in the little boy's section, little kids football uniforms, the helmet, the pads, the jersey and pants, the whole uniform. And you could get the uniform in all the NFL teams. My sister was all in! She had her Miami Dolphins uniform; she had Miami Dolphin wristbands. She had Miami Dolphin socks. She had a little Miami dolphin towel that she tucked in her waistband so she could dry her hands between plays. It was a whole thing!

I will never forget, I walked out of our house one day, and I watched her in her full uniform, threw her football up in the air, catch it, and fall to the ground. And I ran over. Oh my gosh, Lorie, are you okay? Are you okay? She looked at me like I was crazy and said in a very annoyed tone, that she had been tackled. It was hilarious. She just loved all things dolphins.

You know, with little kids, their likes and dislikes tend to come and go? They go through phases of what they like. Not with my sister. She loved dolphins and that stuck with her. So, when she was a few years older, my mom decided it was time to take Lorie to San Diego SeaWorld, so she could see real live dolphins for the very first time. Now, we were living in Bakersfield at the time, so we drove down to San Diego, and we stayed in a hotel the night before. It was a full-on family adventure! My sister was so excited that she was bouncing off the walls. We wake up the crack of dawn the next morning. We get there, and this is a little pro tip, a side note to the story, If you go to San Diego Sea World, and you get to park in the first row, you're there too early. Really, it's unnecessary. We were like the fifth car in the parking lot. But I digress.

We arrive at Sea World, jump out of the car and my sister has my hand on one side and my Mom's hand on the other and she is dragging us straight to the dolphin show. No stops, do not pass go, do not collect $200. I wanted to stop in the gift shops, this was not allowed. Straight to the dolphin show.

Now we're sitting in the stands where the dolphin show is in the arena pool area. We are there so early we are the only people sitting in the stands.

The dolphins weren't even there yet! The trainers have to bring them in from their connecting pools. So we wait. Finally, the trainers bring in the dolphins and start getting everything set up for the show.

Well, one of the trainers spotted my sister from across the pool, and I know I'm partial because she's my sister, and I adore her. But she was a beautiful little girl. She had long, dark, naturally curly hair. It was up in little ponytails, with long ringlet curls, with bows made of red satin ribbons. She was wearing little denim, short overalls. It had a little strawberry patch on the behind. And she's wearing sunglasses, y'all know those big plastic sunglasses kids wear that make them look like a bug? She had her big red bug sunglasses on. She was so cute! Well, one of the trainers spots my sister from across the pool and comes over to her and says, "How would you like to be in the dolphin show? You can feed the dolphin and pet the dolphin!" And my Mom and I, and I'm just like my mother. At the same moment, my mom and I basically screamed, Lorie, you get to be in the dolphin show! You get to feed the dolphin! My sister very calmly looked at the trainer and said, Mm, no. My mom and I were both shocked, what are you talking about? Are you sure? She again, no.

So, my Mom, because she's so shy, said she'll do it. So, my mom got to be in the dolphin show. She was in the whole show. She fed the dolphin, she threw the ball, she petted dolphin, the whole deal.

My sister never said a word about it again until she was a sophomore in high school. One random day, my mom was picking her up from school. She gets in the car, my mom is driving off, so, honey, how was your day? My sister burst into tears. My mom's thinking, oh, gosh, bad day. She asks my sister, "What happened?"

Through my sister's sobs she cried to my Mom saying "I didn't pet the dolphin!" My mom thought, was there a dolphin at school? What was she talking about? San Diego had been years earlier. What was she talking about? But my mom's a good mom. So took my sister and sat her down and asked her what the heck she was talking about. What is going on?

And as my sister cried, she told my mom, she wanted to pet that dolphin so badly. And she had regretted it every day since. My Mom asked her if you wanted to so badly, why didn't you? And she said... because she was afraid. She'd never done that before. What if everybody laughed at her? What if she fell in the water? What if the dolphin bit her? I guess that's just Shamu, but, you know, she was worried. Anyway, she said she was afraid. And because she was afraid, she missed out on what, in her young mind, was the opportunity of a lifetime.

My Mom told my sister that very day, Lorie, your whole entire life, you are going to be presented with opportunities. And with each and every opportunity is going to come a risk. But if you're not willing to take the risk, you're never going to get to take advantage of the opportunities. I think she is very lucky to learn that lesson so young. I think that's a gift. I think most of us learn it much later in life.

My sister, I talk about her like she's a child, she's grown! Remember, I am only 7 years older than her. You should see my sister now. She's a very successful attorney. She has built a multimillion dollar law firm that she started from scratch. She's phenomenal. She is smart and compassionate, an amazing momma, she is just a phenomenal human. It's interesting though. Even as smart and as successful as she is, she still has doubt days. She has down days. But I promise you to this day, when those days happen, all she has to do is call me or call my Mom. And all we have to say to her is, Lorie, you've got to pet your dolphin. And that means that you must take the risk.

I share the story with you because I believe with all my heart and soul that every single one of you reading this book, you have your own dolphin. I don't know what it is. But it is out there, and it is waiting for you. But for you to be able to take advantage of the opportunity, you're going to have to be willing to take the risk.

At some point, you have to stop standing safely on the shore of your own life watching everyone else sail toward their purpose while you convince yourself you are "not ready yet." Ready is overrated. Safe is seductive. And playing small may protect you from failure, criticism, rejection, or discomfort—but it will also rob you of the life you were meant to live and the impact you were created to make. The world does not need more people hiding their gifts, silencing their voices, or waiting for permission to matter. It needs people willing to step forward before they feel fully confident. People willing to take the risk, have the hard conversation, chase the dream, set the boundary, use their voice, lead with courage, and leave a wake worth remembering. Because one day your life will be measured not by how carefully you avoided failure, but by how boldly you showed up, how deeply you loved, how intentionally you lived, and how powerfully you impacted the people around you. So stop shrinking. Stop apologizing for taking up space. Stop talking yourself out of your own greatness. The cape was never the point anyway. Your impact is your superpower. Now go use it.

Go out there and pet your dolphin!

Author Bio

Julie D. Burch is an award-winning keynote speaker, podcaster, author, leadership expert, and professional humorist with more than 28 years of experience helping people communicate more effectively, lead with confidence, and create meaningful impact in both their personal and professional lives.

Known for her signature blend of comedy, candor, and real-world business insight, Julie has built her career on one powerful belief: when people laugh, they listen... and when they listen, they learn. Her "comedy meets content" approach combines practical business strategies, relatable storytelling, hard-earned life lessons, and high-energy humor that leaves audiences both inspired and equipped to take action.

Julie has spoken in all 50 states, three countries, and three U.S. territories—earning frequent flyer miles, standing ovations, and a reputation as one of the most engaging speakers in the industry. In 2017, she was inducted into the SHRM Speaker Hall of Fame at the HR Southwest Conference, and is a sought-after keynote speaker for conferences, corporations, government agencies, educational institutions, and leadership events across the country.

Her client list includes organizations such as Fidelity Investments, Kaiser Permanente, Texas Tech University, the Department of Defense, the EEOC, BP America, the U.S. Army, the U.S. Air Force, and many more. From Fortune 500 companies to nonprofit organizations, Julie is known for connecting with audiences in a way that feels authentic, relatable, practical, and refreshingly real.

In addition to her speaking career, Julie has served on the National Board of Directors for the American Business Women's Association and the Board of Directors for CYT (Christian Youth Theater) of DFW. She is also a frequent presenter and emcee for SHRM national, state, and regional conferences, where her ability to keep audiences energized, engaged, and laughing has made her a trusted industry favorite.

Julie is the co-author of three previous books, including the motivational titles *The Princess Principle* and *Every Heart Has a Gift*, as well as the business-focused *Success Simplified: Simple Solutions, Measurable Results*. Her work consistently centers around empowering people to stop shrinking themselves, communicate courageously, embrace their value, and take back control of their lives.

After years of watching talented, capable people talk themselves out of their own potential, stay silent when they should speak up, and put everyone else's needs ahead of their own, Julie became passionate about one central message: people do not need more potential—they need to recognize the power they already possess.

That belief became the foundation for *Your Impact Is Your Superpower! No Spandex Suit Required.*

Through her writing, speaking, coaching, and leadership work, Julie challenges people to stop self-abdicating, reclaim their voice, and recognize that they already have the ability to create meaningful impact in the lives of those around them.

One of Julie's favorite career highlights was appearing on *Good Morning America*—because apparently the rest of the country needed a little "comedy meets content" too.

Her philosophy is simple: big impact starts with brave choices, honest conversations, and the willingness to stop playing small.

"Solid Business Strategies. Brilliant Comedic Humor."

It's more than a tagline. It's Julie's promise—every single time.

Stay Connected with Julie!

Email:

julie@julieburch.com

Websites:

www.julieburch.com

www.petyourdolphin.com

www.breakthroughwmj.com

Phone:

214.679.2717

Follow Julie on Social!

- **[LinkedIn]** (https://www.linkedin.com/in/julieburchspeaks/)
- **[Facebook]** (https://www.facebook.com/julieburchspeaks/)
- **[X / Twitter]** (https://x.com/thejulieburch)
- **[Instagram]** (https://www.instagram.com/julieburchspeaks/)
- **[TikTok]** (https://www.tiktok.com/@julie.burch.speak)

-**[YouTube]**

(https://www.youtube.com/channel/UCLHH14bdfK6GTn-EryOQtog)

Made in the USA
Coppell, TX
27 May 2026

77883237R00125